50 YEARS OF WEDNESDAY MAGIC

WAWAW

MARTYN LEARY

CONTENTS

Title Page
Preface: Blue and White Until We Die — 1
Chapter 1: When Floodlights Failed — 2
Chapter 2: Jack Whitham's Magical Missing Boots — 3
Chapter 4: The Day We Booed Our Own Team — Then Bought Them Pints — 5
Chapter 5: Boxing Day Massacre — 6
Chapter 6: Jack Charlton's Wild West Wednesday — 7
Chapter 7: Terry Curran and the Flying Goal Celebrations — 8
Chapter 8: Cheap Coach Trips and Illegal Sandwiches — 9
Chapter 9: Ron's White Rolls-Royce and the '91 Promotion Party — 10
Chapter 10: Wembley Wizards — 11
Chapter 11: European Nights and Flat-Cap Diplomacy — 12
Chapter 12: Chris Waddle's Magic Feet and Terrible Hair — 13
Chapter 13: Barry Davies Said It Best — 14
Chapter 14: Sheridan's Shinners and Thunderbolts — 15
Chapter 15: The Relegation Tears — 16
Chapter 16: The Cardiff Miracle — 17
Chapter 17: The 6–0 That Nobody Believed — 18
Chapter 18: Megson's Miracle and the Day the Kop Shook — 19

Chapter 19: Carlos Had A Dream	20
⬜ Part II: Still Wednesday – Still Proud	23
Chapter 20: Josh Windass — The Greatest Header In History	25
Chapter 21: The Goal That Never Was – Crossbar Chaos at Crewe	30
Chapter 22: Kop Kids and School Night Miracles	32
Chapter 23: Diving into Di Canio – Madness, Magic, Mayhem	34
Chapter 24: When the Ref Forgot the Rules – and We Let Him Know	36
Chapter 25: Penalty Curses and Shootout Shocks	38
Chapter 26: Blue Santa, Inflatable Owls & Festive Mayhem	40
Chapter 27: The Shirt That Changed Everything (and Stank for Weeks)	42
Chapter 28: From Megastore to Matchday – Weirdest Club Shop Finds	43
Chapter 29: Owls on Tour – The Time We Got Lost in Luton	45
Chapter 30: The Day It Snowed Inside Hillsborough	47
Chapter 31: 90 Minutes of Rain, 90 Minutes of Singing	49
Chapter 32: The Pie Fell Off My Lap – A Love Story	51
Chapter 33: Singing Through Sorrow – A Tribute to the Fans We Lost	53
Chapter 34: Ball Boys, Banter & That Time One Scored	55
Chapter 35: Wednesday Weddings, Tattoos & Blue Babies	57
Chapter 36: Rivalry Reloaded – Beating Leeds with 10 Men	59
Chapter 37: Matchday Superstitions – Lucky Socks and Weird Routines	61
Chapter 38: When We Took Over Blackpool	63
Chapter 39: Owls Quotes and Sayings – The Gospel According to Hillsborough	65
Chapter 40: Dream Wednesday XI and Closing Words – Once	67

An Owl, Always An Owl

    ☐ Bonus Section: The Blades Banter – Derby Days That Defined Us   77

Chapter 51: The History – 131 Battles, One Divided City   79

Chapter 52: Boxing Day Massacre Revisited – 4–0 and Still Glorious   81

Chapter 53: When the Ref Was Red and So Were We   83

Chapter 54: Blades in Disguise – The Wednesday Players They Tried to Steal   85

Chapter 55: The Best Wednesday Goals vs United (Ranked by Cheek & Chaos)   87

Chapter 56: Red Cards, Rain Delays & Riot Vans – The Wildest Derby Days   89

Chapter 57: Heroes of the Hillsborough Half – Our Derby Day Legends   91

Chapter 58: "Mind the Gap!" and Other Famous Chants That Drove Them Mad   93

Chapter 59: The One Where They Thought They Had Us   95

Chapter 60: It's More Than Football – Why the Derby Really Matters   97

Page 1: Fan Voices – From Hillsborough to the World   99

Page 2: A Wednesday Bucket List   101

Page 3: Letter to My Younger Wednesday Self   102

Page 4: The Hillsborough Soundtrack – Music That Made Us   103

Page 5: Matchday Memes & Wednesday Banter   105

Page 6: Why We Still Believe   107

PREFACE: BLUE AND WHITE UNTIL WE DIE

Supporting Sheffield Wednesday isn't just a choice — it's something stitched into your soul, passed down like a family heirloom, or discovered like a calling you never knew you were waiting for. It's the flutter in your chest as the players walk out at Hillsborough. It's the heartbreak that lingers after a crushing relegation. It's the unshakable pride you feel when thousands belt out *Hi Ho Silver Lining* in one defiant, glorious voice.

This book isn't a history lesson. It's not just stats and scorelines. It's a tribute — to the people, the places, the songs, the heartbreaks, and the moments that make up what it means to be Wednesday.

It's about standing soaked on the terraces in the freezing rain, knowing full well the lads might let you down — but turning up anyway, because that's what we do. It's about the magical chaos of away days, the characters you meet, and the stories you tell again and again. It's about the thunder of a goal in the last minute. The silence after a crushing loss. The belief that, somehow, we'll rise again.

Inside these pages are fifty years of laughter, pride, passion and pain — as seen through the eyes of those who lived it. The foggy madness of Chesterfield. The Boxing Day massacre. Charlton's chaos. Windass' wonder. And everything in between.

To be Wednesday is to believe — when nobody else does. To sing, even in the silence. To wear your colours with a grin and a growl. This is our story. And it's one we never stop telling.

Because we are Wednesday.

And we always will be.

— *Martyn Leary*

CHAPTER 1: WHEN FLOODLIGHTS FAILED

The Great Fog Match at Chesterfield (1972)

You never forget your first taste of madness.

It was 1972. Chesterfield away. A fog thick enough to choke a coal miner, and a pitch you couldn't see from twenty yards away — but that didn't stop us. Hundreds of Wednesdayites packed onto creaky old coaches with paper-thin windows and dodgy heaters, clutching rattles, flasks of soup, and that eternal sense of belief: *This is our week.*

By kickoff, visibility was somewhere between "bad" and "are we even still at a football match?" You'd hear a roar and have no idea which team had scored. One bloke near us swore blind he saw Peter Eustace volley one in from the halfway line. Turns out it hit a steward.

Players were shadows. The ball disappeared like a magic trick. It was chaos. Beautiful, ludicrous, freezing chaos.

We lost, of course. Or won. No one really knows. But it didn't matter. What mattered was that we were *there*. That we sang through the fog, through the cold, through the nonsense. And as the final whistle blew — or at least we think it did — a chant rose from the mist: *"We are Wednesday, say we are Wednesday!"*

It was our first taste of the surreal and stubborn loyalty that defines this club. When the world goes dark, Wednesdayites still turn up.

Fog or not, we never stop believing.

CHAPTER 2: JACK WHITHAM'S MAGICAL MISSING BOOTS

(1971)

Jack Whitham was a striker built like a rock and blessed with a hammer of a right foot. In 1971, he was Wednesday's great hope — a lad who could score goals from angles that barely existed.

And one foggy afternoon at Hillsborough, he made club folklore... by misplacing his boots.

Legend goes that Jack turned up just before kickoff, only to realise his boots had vanished. Not left at home. *Vanished.* Vanished like socks in the wash or leads in injury time. Cue panic. Cue chaos. Cue some poor kit lad legging it down Penistone Road searching for a size ten.

But this was Jack Whitham — a man who could make magic out of madness. Someone finally turned up with a mismatched pair — one black Puma, one old Mitre. Didn't matter. Jack laced them up, jogged out five minutes late, and within ten minutes he'd scored twice.

The crowd roared like it was a cup final. One lad shouted, *"He should lose his boots every week!"* and the Kop exploded.

That day, Jack became a legend not just for his goals — but for proving that nothing, not even a missing pair of boots, could stop a true Wednesday warrior.

Because when you wear the blue and white, you play with heart — even if your feet don't match.

Chapter 3: Hillsborough's Hard Men

Playing Through Mud and Murder (1975)

Back in the '70s, football wasn't polished. It was muddy, brutal, and glorious.

And at Hillsborough, we had our own version of trench warfare every Saturday.

Pitches? More like cow fields. Tackles? Less "sliding" and more "assassination attempts." Shin pads were optional. Teeth? Not guaranteed. But the lads that pulled on that Wednesday shirt played like gladiators — even when it looked more like rugby than football.

In 1975, we had a spine of players you'd cross the street to avoid. Tommy Craig — silky when he wanted to be, savage when he had to be. Peter Shirtliff — would tackle a steam train and come away with the ball. And then there was Mel Sterland, who once got kicked in the head, spat out blood, and played on like he'd just sneezed.

That season was chaos. We weren't winning much, but the tackles were thunder, and the crowd loved it. One match, a young lad behind me shouted, *"Break his legs!"* His gran told him off — not for the violence, but for swearing.

That's what it was. Hillsborough was our battleground. A sacred mess of mud, magic, and menace. Every blade of grass had history in it. And when our lads went in for a 50/50, you knew it was going to be a 100/0 in our favour.

They weren't just hard. They were ours.

CHAPTER 4: THE DAY WE BOOED OUR OWN TEAM — THEN BOUGHT THEM PINTS

(1976)

Only Wednesday fans could pull off something as beautifully bizarre as this.

It was 1976. Expectations were high. Spirits were low. We were at home to Shrewsbury — yes, *Shrewsbury* — and the football was flatter than a pub shandy. Passes going backwards, tackles missed, heads down. The Kop tried to lift them. But after 80 minutes of misery, patience snapped.

The boos started in the North Stand. Then the South joined in. Finally, the Kop — our sacred choir — let rip. It was righteous. Loud. Honest. We *loved* the club... and we hated what we were watching.

Then something weird happened.

After the match, a few players ended up in a pub near Hillsborough Corner — probably trying to hide. But instead of turning on them, fans started buying them pints. Proper Yorkshire logic: *"You were rubbish... but you're still one of us. Get this down ya."*

One old bloke told the left-back, *"You couldn't trap a bag of cement, lad. But you'll be better next week. You've got to be."*

That was the beauty of it. We were honest. Brutal when needed. But loyal beyond reason. We'd boo you off, then buy you a drink. Because deep down, we knew they cared as much as we did — they were just having a stinker.

And that, in a nutshell, is what it means to be Wednesday.

CHAPTER 5: BOXING DAY MASSACRE

1979's Eternal Glory

If you ask any Wednesdayite over the age of 40 about *the* game, they won't say Wembley. They won't say Cardiff.
They'll say **Boxing Day. 1979. 4–0. Against them.**

Sheffield United came to Hillsborough full of confidence. They were ahead of us in the table. Their fans were loud, cocky, and singing like they'd already won. But what they didn't know was that they were walking straight into a massacre — the most delicious kind.

We battered them. *Absolutely destroyed them.* It was 4–0, but it could've been 7. Terry Curran ran riot. Ian Mellor tore their back line to shreds. The third goal was like watching Brazil — in S6.

The noise that day still echoes. Ask anyone who was there — the Kop didn't just sing, it **erupted**. It was a party, a statement, a demolition job wrapped in blue and white ribbons.

And the Blades? Shell-shocked. Silenced. Some even left before halftime. They'd turned up expecting dominance and left with bruises on their pride that still haven't healed.

We've had big wins before. And since. But nothing — *nothing* — will ever match the sweet taste of that Boxing Day bloodbath. It wasn't just a win. It was **our day**.

Etched in memory. Tattooed on the soul.

CHAPTER 6: JACK CHARLTON'S WILD WEST WEDNESDAY

(1978–1983)

Jack Charlton didn't manage a football club. He *invaded* it.

When Big Jack arrived in 1977, we were in the footballing wilderness. Morale low. Squad average. Fans loyal, but starved. What we needed wasn't just a manager — we needed a sheriff.

And Big Jack was perfect. Towering. Straight-talking. Didn't give a toss about reputations. Within months, he'd turned our squad into a team of hard-working, no-nonsense brawlers with a sprinkle of flair.

Tactics? Simple. *Get it forward. Win it back. Do it again.* But it worked. Players loved him or feared him — sometimes both. One training session, he threw a player's boots into the Don after a sloppy pass. "If you can't find a teammate," he said, "maybe the ducks will."

Under Jack, Hillsborough became a fortress. The crowd believed again. Games were ugly, but glorious. Blood and thunder football. Long throws, crunching tackles, goals off knees and elbows — and we **loved** it.

Promotion in '80 was wild. Pubs overflowed. Coaches roared into town with blue and white flags waving out the windows. One fan got "Charlton's Army" tattooed on his chest with a biro and a sewing needle. Commitment.

He left in '83, but he never really left our hearts. Jack didn't just manage Wednesday — he *woke it up*.

He gave us belief. And he gave us barmy memories that still make us grin like idiots.

CHAPTER 7: TERRY CURRAN AND THE FLYING GOAL CELEBRATIONS

(1979)

Terry Curran didn't just play football. He *performed* it.

When he pulled on the Wednesday shirt, you knew something special might happen. A cheeky backheel, a mazy run through three defenders, a thunderous finish — and then... the celebration.

He didn't do boring fist pumps. Terry **took off** like Concorde. Arms out, chin up, bombing down the touchline like a lad trying to get served first at the pub. Every goal was a spectacle — not just for what he did with the ball, but what he did *after* it hit the net.

Fans didn't just cheer when he scored — we *chased* him, laughing, roaring, some even running down the front rows to join in the madness. His flying celebration became iconic. It wasn't just about goals. It was about joy. Pure, unfiltered, blue-and-white joy.

Curran was electric. Sometimes he went missing for 30 minutes... then BANG — goal from nowhere. He was unpredictable, outrageous, and ours.

Ask any old-school Wednesdayite, and they'll tell you: Terry Curran didn't just score in the Massacre... he *owned* it.

To this day, if you listen closely on a Boxing Day, you can still hear the crowd shouting *"GO ON, TERRY!"* as he soars down that wing, arms wide like a lad chasing a dream — and catching it.

CHAPTER 8: CHEAP COACH TRIPS AND ILLEGAL SANDWICHES

(Every Away Day Ever)

Ah, away days. Glorious, grimy, glorious again.

They weren't just about football — they were about **ritual**. A dodgy coach that smelt of crisps and fags. A 4 a.m. meet at the train station car park. Someone always forgetting their ticket. Someone else bringing an entire crate of beer "for hydration."

And the sandwiches — dear God, the sandwiches.

Not from a shop. No. From someone's mum. Wrapped in cling film. Ham, cheese, possibly both. Sometimes with *mystery meat* and a note that said "don't swap with strangers." But we swapped anyway. It was tradition.

And we did it for Grimsby. For Cambridge. For Rochdale on a Tuesday night in the freezing rain, where we lost 1–0 to a penalty no one saw and still sang all the way home.

Coach windows would steam up from laughter. Lads passed around fanzines, tinnies, and horror stories from '88. One trip to Port Vale, we broke down on the M1. Instead of complaining, someone started chanting *"We're on the way to nowhere!"* and it became a classic.

Away days were chaos. They still are. But that's the magic.

Because it's not always about the result. It's about the *ride* — the mates, the memories, the madness. And those sandwiches.

CHAPTER 9: RON'S WHITE ROLLS-ROYCE AND THE '91 PROMOTION PARTY

(1990–1991)

If Jack Charlton brought grit, **Big Ron** brought the glitter.

When Ron Atkinson rocked up at Hillsborough in 1989, it felt like Hollywood had arrived in S6. Big coats, big cigars, big confidence. He didn't just manage a football club — he *owned the room*. And he drove a white Rolls-Royce that looked like it belonged on a Bond film set.

But here's the thing: he could **manage**, too.

Ron took a team drifting in Division Two and turned them into artists. John Sheridan pulling strings. Hirsty bullying defenders. Waddle whispering to the ball like it was a lover. And behind it all, Ron, strutting down the touchline like a man with the ending already written.

And what an ending it was.

Promotion in 1991 was as beautiful as it was bonkers. Hillsborough rocking. Fans crying. Scarves twirling like propellers. Ron's grin bigger than ever. And that night — the party spilled into every corner of the city.

One bloke turned up at The Wicker with a plastic owl on his head and said, *"We're flying again, lads!"*

We didn't just go up. We *arrived*. Ron gave us swagger, silverware, and stories we're still telling.

And that white Rolls-Royce? Still the sexiest car to ever roll through the Hillsborough gates.

CHAPTER 10: WEMBLEY WIZARDS

The 1991 League Cup Final

Some matches make history. Others become **legend**.

In April 1991, Sheffield Wednesday — a second division side — walked out at Wembley to face Manchester United. Ferguson's United. The favourites. The money. The media darlings.

But they didn't have *us*.

We took over Wembley that day. Blue and white everywhere. Flags, face paint, inflatable owls, and fans roaring like we were going to war.

The game? Electric. United came at us hard, but we stood firm. Then, in the 37th minute, the moment.

Sheridan. The Shinner Heard Round The World. A scuffed strike, bobbling, bouncing, but glorious. It hit the net and **Wembley exploded**.

The rest of the game was pure noise. Passion. Panic. Belief. And when the whistle blew... we'd done it.
Wednesday 1 — Manchester United 0.
League Cup Winners. In style. In heart. In **history**.

Players collapsed to their knees. Fans danced in the aisles. Big Ron lit up a cigar the size of a trombone.

That wasn't just a cup win. It was a message.

We're Wednesday. And we belong on the biggest stage.

CHAPTER 11: EUROPEAN NIGHTS AND FLAT-CAP DIPLOMACY

(1992)

For years, we'd sung about being a "big club." In 1992, we proved it — on the **continent**.

Europe. Proper Europe. Not a pre-season in Marbella. We were in the **UEFA Cup**, mixing it with the big boys. And while our passports were dusty, our pride was polished. Sheffield Wednesday were back — and international.

We faced teams like Spora Luxembourg and FC Kaiserslautern. Proper clubs with names that sounded like Bond villains. But we travelled in numbers — flat caps, pint pots, and Union Jacks scrawled with *"Wednesday 'Til I Die."*

One lad got stopped at customs in Belgium because he tried to smuggle in a crate of Henderson's Relish. Another got lost in a German beer hall and turned up 20 minutes into the game... somehow wearing lederhosen.

But it wasn't just about the comedy. We played **brilliant** football. Slick passing. Steel in midfield. Confidence up front. And the fans? Unbelievable. Singing in broken German. Teaching locals about chip butties.

We didn't win the cup. But we won **respect**. And we proved we belonged on Europe's stage.

For a few glorious months, Hillsborough wasn't just a fortress — it was the home of continental dreams, kebab-fuelled away days, and the finest fans this side of the Rhine.

CHAPTER 12: CHRIS WADDLE'S MAGIC FEET AND TERRIBLE HAIR

(1992–1993)

There are legends... and then there's **Chris Waddle**.

By the time he joined Wednesday, Waddle had already done it all — Marseille, Spurs, England. But no one expected *magic*. And certainly not magic wrapped in a mullet.

He arrived in 1992 looking like he'd just stepped out of a Top of the Pops blooper reel. But give him the ball... and he **danced**. Glided. Jinked. He made defenders look like they were wearing roller skates.

And Hillsborough? Fell in love instantly.

Every time he touched the ball, there was a buzz. A flick here, a dummy there, a cross that curved like poetry. He didn't run — he *floated*. Like someone had buttered his boots and told gravity to have a day off.

1993 was peak Waddle. Cup finals. Goals. That performance against Sheffield United in the FA Cup semi — a **masterclass**. He was untouchable. Unplayable. *Unreal.*

And the hair? Glorious. Business at the front, party at the back. Kids copied it. Adults feared it. But no one dared question it — because it belonged to **the most gifted footballer Hillsborough had seen in a generation**.

Chris Waddle reminded us that football wasn't just a battle — it could be **beautiful**.

CHAPTER 13: BARRY DAVIES SAID IT BEST

"You Have To Say, That's Magnificent!"

Commentary can elevate a moment. But *only* if the moment's worth it.

Wembley, 1993. FA Cup Semi-Final. Wednesday vs Sheffield United — the Steel City Showdown on football's grandest stage. Tense. Tight. Gritty. And then came the moment that shook the nation.

Chris Waddle picked up the ball in midfield. Swivel. Shimmy. Laid it off. A few passes later, it came back to him. One touch. Then… *bang* — a strike that bent physics and belief, straight into the top corner.

The Wednesday end **exploded**. Blue and white limbs everywhere. Tears, beers, screams. And on BBC One, in front of millions, Barry Davies dropped a line that became *immortal*:

"You have to say, that's magnificent."

Six simple words. But they captured **everything**. The goal. The game. The moment. The magic of Waddle.

Commentators dream of moments like that. We **lived** one.

It wasn't just the goal that was magnificent. It was the roar. The occasion. The city split in two — and Wednesday rising above.

Barry got it spot on.

And every time you hear that line today, a little piece of your soul swells up and whispers: *we were magnificent that day.*

CHAPTER 14: SHERIDAN'S SHINNERS AND THUNDERBOLTS

John Sheridan never looked like a footballer.

Bit stocky. Bit scruffy. Hair like he cut it himself with garden shears. But give him a ball… and *watch the magic unfold.*

He was part sniper, part streetfighter. He didn't just play midfield — he **owned** it. Sprayed passes like poetry. And every now and then, he'd unleash a **thunderbolt** so pure it could split the crossbar in half.

And then there were the *shinners.*

He had this weird knack for scoring with the part of the leg most players avoid — that no-man's-land between knee and ankle. They weren't pretty. But they *flew in.* Sliced. Skewed. Somehow unstoppable.

Ask any fan to name a classic Sheri goal and they'll pause. Not because there's none — but because **there are too many**.

The 1991 League Cup Final winner? That wasn't a shinner. That was a memory carved in silver. Cool, controlled, clinical — the stuff dreams are made of.

He wasn't flash. He wasn't loud. He just ran the show like a conductor in mud-stained boots.

And when he left, we didn't just lose a player. We lost the **heartbeat** of the midfield.

Sheridan goals were like takeaway curry. Maybe not elegant, but full of heat, unforgettable, and exactly what you needed on a cold Wednesday night.

CHAPTER 15: THE RELEGATION TEARS

2000

The year 2000 wasn't just the turn of a century. For Wednesdayites, it felt like the end of the world.

We'd been hanging on by our fingertips — poor form, boardroom chaos, the spark fizzling out. But in our hearts, we still believed. We always believe.

Until that day in May.

It wasn't dramatic. It wasn't glorious failure. It was cold, slow heartbreak. Relegation confirmed with a whimper. Fans didn't scream. They *sobbed*. Grown men with scarves covering their eyes. Kids asking their dads why everyone looked so sad.

The worst part? The silence. Hillsborough, usually full of defiance, was still. No chants. Just the sound of a dream slipping away.

And yet — even in that moment — there was love.

Players clapped the crowd. The crowd clapped back. Some in anger, some in sorrow, but most out of **loyalty**. Because this wasn't just about a football team. It was about identity.

We were going down. But we weren't going anywhere.

That's what separates us. Through the tears, we still stood. Still wore the colours. Still believed that one day, the good times would return.

And they did. Because we **never stop loving this club** — even when it breaks our hearts.

CHAPTER 16: THE CARDIFF MIRACLE

2005 Playoff Final

Fast forward five years. Cardiff. Playoff Final. League One. One game to climb out of the muck.

And as always — Wednesdayites turned up in force.

The Millennium Stadium was painted blue and white. Flags waving. Chants echoing off the roof. Nerves jangling like pocket change on a rollercoaster.

Against Hartlepool, of all teams. A decent side. No fear. No fuss. And after 82 minutes... *we were losing*. 2–1. Gutted.

Then came the madness.

Goals from nowhere. Passes laced with destiny. Players running on fumes, tackling like it was life or death. Chris Brunt weaving magic. Steve MacLean slotting in the coolest penalty of his life. The crowd — delirious.

Final score: **4–2 after extra time**.

Tears again. But this time, tears of **pure joy**.

Kids lifted on shoulders. Strangers hugging. Grown men jumping into fountains. One bloke proposed to his girlfriend outside the stadium, using his match ticket as a ring box. She said yes. *Obviously.*

That day, we didn't just win promotion. We reclaimed **belief**.

Cardiff wasn't just a final. It was a reminder that no matter how dark it gets, Wednesday always finds a way to rise again.

CHAPTER 17: THE 6–0 THAT NOBODY BELIEVED

Southampton at Hillsborough (2010)

Sometimes a match feels like a dream. Other times it feels like someone spiked your Bovril.

Wednesday 6, Southampton 0. Yes — that happened. Yes — we played like world-beaters. And no — most of us didn't believe it until we read the papers the next morning.

It was March 2010. Southampton were flying. We were floundering. Another grey afternoon at Hillsborough. Expectation low. Hope, even lower.

And then... **BOOM.**

Jermaine Johnson turned into prime Ronaldinho. Marcus Tudgay was scoring like it was a testimonial. Every pass stuck. Every shot flew in. Fans were looking at each other like, *"Is this a prank?"*

By halftime, it was 3–0. By full-time, it was **six**. SIX. Against one of the best teams in the league. Their fans looked like they'd seen a ghost. Ours looked like they'd won the lottery.

And the noise? Glorious. Pure, unfiltered shock and joy. A proper "I was there" moment.

It didn't fix everything. We still had struggles to come. But for those 90 minutes, Hillsborough was a cathedral of madness, and we were witnessing football from another universe.

Even now, some fans think it was a dream. But we were there. We saw it.

And we'll never let anyone forget it.

CHAPTER 18: MEGSON'S MIRACLE AND THE DAY THE KOP SHOOK

2012

If ever a man embodied Sheffield Wednesday, it was **Gary Megson**.

Born a Wednesdayite. Played for us. Bled for us. Came back to manage with fire in his belly and unfinished business in his eyes. He didn't just want promotion — he wanted to do it **for us**.

And in 2012, he gave us one of the most unforgettable wins of the modern era — **The Steel City Derby**.

United were flying high. Arrogant. Loud. They'd beaten us at the Lane. But this was Hillsborough. **Our turf. Our noise. Our moment.**

That atmosphere... electric. The Kop didn't just sing — it **shook**. The whole ground rattled with rage, revenge, and raw belief.

And then Reda Johnson rose like a skyscraper to put us ahead. And the place **erupted**. Chairs flying. Beers in the air. Old fellas crying. You could feel the roof lift off.

We won. 1–0. A result that shifted the season. Gave us momentum. Gave us hope. Gave us pride.

Megson didn't finish the job — cruelly sacked just after. But that win? That day? That **derby**?

He'll always have that. And we'll always thank him for reminding us what it means to be **proper Wednesday**.

CHAPTER 19: CARLOS HAD A DREAM

The Premier League Nearly Boys (2016)

Carlos Carvalhal arrived with charm, eyebrows of destiny, and a clipboard full of dreams.

No one expected much — just a bit of stability. Maybe a playoff push if the stars aligned. What we got instead was something close to **magic**.

Carlos turned Wednesday into a team with swagger. Barry Bannan pulling strings. Forestieri firing on all cylinders. Kieran Lee — the silent assassin. And a Hillsborough crowd that suddenly believed **again**.

2016 wasn't just about results. It was about a feeling — that Wednesday were **back**.

We finished 6th and made it to the playoff final at Wembley. Tens of thousands of us descended on London. Blue and white everywhere. Flags in car windows, owls on every lamp post. The walk down Wembley Way was like something from a film.

We lost to Hull. One moment of brilliance from Diame. That's all it took. And yeah — it hurt. It *really* hurt.

But you know what? We didn't walk away broken. We walked away **proud**.

Because Carlos had a dream. And for a while, so did we.

We remembered who we were. We remembered that Wednesday didn't just belong in the big games — we *lit them up*.

And we sang his song long after he'd gone.

> *Carlos had a dream… to build a football team…*

And in our hearts, he did.

PART II: STILL WEDNESDAY – STILL PROUD

21. The Goal That Never Was – Crossbar Chaos at Crewe
22. Kop Kids and School Night Miracles
23. Diving into Di Canio – Madness, Magic, Mayhem
24. When the Ref Forgot the Rules – and We Let Him Know
25. Penalty Curses and Shootout Shocks
26. Blue Santa, Inflatable Owls & Festive Mayhem
27. The Shirt That Changed Everything (and Stank for Weeks)
28. From Megastore to Matchday – Weirdest Club Shop Finds
29. Owls on Tour: The Time We Got Lost in Luton
30. The Day It Snowed Inside Hillsborough
31. 90 Minutes of Rain, 90 Minutes of Singing
32. The Pie Fell Off My Lap – A Love Story
33. Singing Through Sorrow – A Tribute to the Fans We Lost
34. Ball Boys, Banter & That Time One Scored
35. Wednesday Weddings, Tattoos & Blue Babies
36. Rivalry Reloaded – Beating Leeds with 10 Men
37. From Radio Rentals to Sky Sports – Watching the Owls Evolve
38. When We Took Over Blackpool
39. Matchday Superstitions – Lucky Socks and Weird Routines
40. One of Our Own – When a Fan Made the

MARTYN LEARY

Bench

CHAPTER 20: JOSH WINDASS — THE GREATEST HEADER IN HISTORY

Wembley, 2023

Some moments are so perfect, so absurd, so storybook — you'd think they were scripted by the gods.

Wembley. 2023. Playoff final. 123rd minute.

We all know what came before: the impossible comeback against Peterborough in the semi. The 4–0. The penalty drama. The belief *only Wednesday fans* could carry after years of madness.

And now — **Barnsley**. Cagey. Tense. Nasty at times. Extra time. Nerves shredded.

And then came **the cross**.

And then came **Windass**.

Time slowed. He flew through the air like a man possessed. A diving header. Last kick of the game. Ball smashes into the net.

GOAL.

And then? **Carnage.**

Wembley exploded. Flares. Screams. People flying. One bloke threw his shoe and never got it back. Another passed out from joy. Josh Windass did what his dad once did — score at Wembley. But this one? This was **ours**.

Fans collapsed in tears. Strangers hugged like family. That header wasn't just a goal. It was **redemption**.

It was everything we've waited for.

Wednesday were going up.
And in the most Sheffield Wednesday way possible — **drama**,

chaos, and glory in the very last second.

Josh Windass gave us a moment that will outlive us all.

You'll tell your grandkids about that header.

And they'll wish they'd seen it too.

Bonus Sections

Favourite Sheffield Wednesday Matches

A collection of fan-submitted favourites:

- *Boxing Day Massacre (1979)*
- *Wembley League Cup Final (1991)*
- *The 4–2 Cardiff Playoff Comeback (2005)*
- *The Peterborough Miracle (2023)*
- *6–0 vs Southampton (2010)*

Each one unforgettable. Each one a badge of honour.

Legends of Hillsborough

Just a few names carved into the soul of S6:

- **Chris Waddle**
- **David Hirst**
- **Roland Nilsson**
- **John Sheridan**
- **Mel Sterland**
- **Reda Johnson**
- **Lee Bullen**
- **Barry Bannan**
- **Josh Windass**

Heroes all. Past and present, boots filled with pride.

Your Memories of Hillsborough (Write Your Own)

This space is for *you*. Write in the margins. Tell your story.

- Your first game.
- The player that made you fall in love.
- The moment you cried — for joy or heartbreak.

This book isn't finished without your voice.

My First Match

Blank page for every fan to remember that magic day. Write:

- Date:
- Opponent:
- Score:
- Who took you:
- What you wore:
- What you'll never forget:

Because your first match lives forever.

Top 10 Wednesday Goals

In no particular order, and always debated:

1. Waddle vs United (1993 FA Cup Semi-Final)
2. Sheridan vs Man Utd (1991 League Cup Final)
3. Windass vs Barnsley (2023 Playoff Final)
4. Hirst vs Derby (screamer, 1990)
5. Brunt's curler vs Leeds
6. Reda Johnson's bullet header
7. Forestieri vs Derby (2015)
8. Bannan's volley vs Huddersfield
9. Reach's thunderbolt vs Leeds
10. Tudgay's chip at Hillsborough

Agree? Argue? Add your own.

Great Wednesday Managers

- Jack Charlton – The Enforcer
- Ron Atkinson – The Showman
- Trevor Francis – The Quiet Architect
- Carlos Carvalhal – The Dreamer
- Darren Moore – The Believer

Each one gave us something to hold onto.

Favourite Away Days

From Bradford's frozen steps to Wembley Way, Wednesdayites have *been there, done that, sang through it.*
Memorable mentions:

- Chesterfield, 1972 (fog and mystery)
- Cardiff, 2005 (playoff magic)
- Brentford, 2014 (promotion party)
- Hull, 2016 (painful, but proud)
- Peterborough, 2023 (resurrection)

Owls Quotes and Sayings

- "We are Wednesday, aren't we?"
- "Through rain, sleet, and relegation — I turn up."
- "Hi Ho Silver Lining — louder than life."
- "There's only one club in Sheffield."
- "I was born Wednesday. I'll die Wednesday."

Tattoo-worthy. Chant-worthy. True.

Dream Wednesday XI

Formation: 4-4-2 (classic, of course)

- **GK:** Kevin Pressman
- **RB:** Roland Nilsson
- **CB:** Des Walker
- **CB:** Reda Johnson

- **LB:** Nigel Worthington
- **RM:** Chris Waddle
- **CM:** John Sheridan
- **CM:** Barry Bannan
- **LM:** Chris Brunt
- **ST:** David Hirst
- **ST:** Jermaine Johnson (for chaos)

Subs: Bullen, Forestieri, Carbone, Harkes, Di Canio (just for the drama)

Closing Words: Once An Owl, Always An Owl

This book isn't just about football.
It's about **family**, memory, loyalty, and love.
It's for the cold nights, the lost voices, the lifelong mates made on the terraces.
It's for the highs that make you float, and the lows that make you stronger.
It's for the scarves hung in back windows.
For the flags in the garage.
For the name "Wednesday" that means more than any other word.

You're part of this story.

Because whether you were there in '79 or just found the club last year...
You get it.
You *feel* it.

And you always will.

Up the Owls. Always.

CHAPTER 21: THE GOAL THAT NEVER WAS – CROSSBAR CHAOS AT CREWE

Crewe Alexandra away. Cold Tuesday night. Mid-table. Barely a whisper in the national press. But for the 1,200 Wednesdayites crammed into that tiny away stand, it turned into **folklore**.

We were chasing a play-off spot, needing a spark. The match was tight — scrappy in the middle, few chances, a ref who'd left his cards in the car. And then it happened.

Second half. A quick counter. Our winger (I won't name names, but you know the one with pace and a right foot like Thor's hammer) cut inside and smashed a screamer from 25 yards. It dipped like a stone skipping across water — smacked the underside of the bar and bounced *down*.

Over the line. CLEARLY over the line.

The away end went **ballistic**. We were jumping, hugging, piling onto the rows in front. One lad screamed so loud he lost a filling. The chants rang out: *"1–0 to the Super Owls!"* followed by *"You don't know what you're doing!"* — aimed squarely at the ref and his mate with the flag who apparently blinked through the most obvious goal in lower-league history.

Play went on. Crewe hoofed it clear. The ref gave nothing.

By full-time, we'd drawn 0–0 and the entire fanbase had entered the five stages of grief. On the coach home, we watched the footage on someone's cracked iPhone — clear as anything. Ball. Over the line. Keeper scrambling in vain. A travesty.

Even the next day, TalkSport picked it up. "Travelling Wednesday fans robbed," they said. No apology. No points. Just the sweet, sour taste of injustice.

But here's the thing: we *never* forgot. That match became a badge of honour. A story we still tell.

Because at Wednesday, we don't just remember the wins — we remember the **robberies**, too. We wear them like scars.

And you better believe next time we go to Crewe, we'll still be singing *"It was OVER the line!"* from the first minute to the last.

CHAPTER 22: KOP KIDS AND SCHOOL NIGHT MIRACLES

There's something mythic about your **first night under the lights**. For most of us, it starts the same way — begging your mum, bribing your dad, or getting your nan to say, "He's old enough now."

It's midweek. School in the morning. You've got spelling tests, or science homework you haven't touched. But none of that matters.

Because tonight, you're going to **Hillsborough**.

I remember my first. November, late 90s. Rain in the air. Fog clinging to the roofs of the houses. Dad picked me up early from school and said, *"Get changed. We're off to the match."* No better sentence in the English language.

We sat in the South Stand, halfway up, me clutching a sausage roll and a programme like it was gold. The lights hit the pitch like a film set. The players looked taller, sharper. The ball moved faster. Everything was **magnified**.

That night, we played Sunderland. We were losing. I didn't care — I was just staring at the players in awe. But then, with minutes to go, Andy Booth rose like a steam engine and headed one in. The place *shook*.

It wasn't just a goal — it was **electricity**. I jumped, I screamed, I didn't even notice my sausage roll fly two rows ahead.

On the way home, Dad bought me chips and a can of Tango. I told him I wanted to be David Hirst when I grew up. He told me, "You better learn to run first."

The next day at school, I couldn't concentrate. I drew the scoreline in the back of my maths book and got a detention. Miss Hughes said football wasn't everything. I disagreed.

Ask any Wednesday fan about their first night game and they'll remember *everything*. The walk up Penistone Road. The steam from the burger vans. The way the floodlights turned our pitch into a stage.

Because when you fall in love with Wednesday, it's usually **under the lights**, wrapped in your dad's coat, singing when your voice still squeaks.

You're not just watching football. You're becoming part of a story that started long before you — and will go on long after.

CHAPTER 23: DIVING INTO DI CANIO
– MADNESS, MAGIC, MAYHEM

Paolo Di Canio was like a firework in a dressing room full of candles — dazzling, dangerous, and absolutely impossible to ignore.

When he arrived in 1997, he brought with him a touch of Italian flair, a sprinkle of genius… and a full trolley of *emotional baggage*. But my word, could he play.

He didn't just control the ball — he *seduced* it. Flicks, dribbles, dummies, shots from impossible angles. Fans gasped. Defenders spun. And commentators ran out of adjectives.

He was box-office, every single week.

But with Paolo, brilliance always came with baggage. If you weren't giving him the ball, he'd let you know. If the ref gave a throw-in the wrong way, he'd be on the verge of revolution. If the wind blew the wrong way — arms flailed, eyebrows twitched, and tantrums followed.

Then came **The Push**.

Arsenal. Hillsborough. 1998. Referee Paul Alcock gives Di Canio a red card after a flare-up. Paolo's response? He *shoves the ref*. Alcock stumbles backwards like he's been shot by a cannon. Crowd in stunned silence. Alan Hansen probably fell off his chair.

It was madness. But it was **classic Di Canio**. No half-measures. He left the club soon after, but his memory — and that moment — stuck around like a tattoo you can't laser off.

Ask any Wednesday fan, and you'll hear the same mix of awe and agony: "Paolo was mental… but he was *ours* for a bit."

For that brief spell, we had one of the most gifted, volatile players in world football wearing blue and white.

And like any great rockstar — he burnt bright, fast, and unforgettable.

CHAPTER 24: WHEN THE REF FORGOT THE RULES – AND WE LET HIM KNOW

Some matches are classics. Others are catastrophes.
And then there are those matches where the *referee becomes the main event* — for all the wrong reasons.

It was a scrappy away fixture. One of those matches you don't even remember who we were playing — only that the man in black made himself the star of the show.

It started harmlessly. A few soft bookings. The odd foul that got waved away. But then it turned into a **comedy of errors**. Throw-ins given the wrong way. Advantage played when no foul had occurred. At one point, he forgot to restart the game after a substitution and the players just stood there staring at him.

And then came the moment we'll never forget.

Their striker went down in the box like he'd been tasered. No contact. Not even close. We expected a yellow for diving. Instead — **penalty**.

The away end *erupted*. Chant after chant rained down:

> "The referee's from Doncaster!"
> "You don't know what you're doing!"
> "You're worse than Mike Dean!"
> And the classic: *"VAR! VAR! VAR!"* — even though League One barely had working floodlights, let alone video replays.

But then — in a moment of pure farce — he let **the wrong player take the penalty**. Their lad stepped up, scored… and only then did the lino say, "He wasn't on the pitch when it was awarded."

Chaos.

Play was halted. Managers screaming. Fans losing it. One Wednesdayite in a high-vis vest tried to show the ref a rulebook from his coat pocket. Security stopped him. Hero, though.

The goal stood. We lost. But no one left early — because we were watching the most hilariously bad officiating masterclass in the history of modern football.

It reminded us of something crucial:
Football is heartbreak. But it's also pantomime.
And no one enjoys both like a Wednesdayite.

CHAPTER 25: PENALTY CURSES AND SHOOTOUT SHOCKS

If there's one thing guaranteed to make a Wednesdayite sweat, shake, or temporarily lose their faith in the universe — it's a **penalty shootout**.

We've been through them all.
The hopeful ones. The heartbreaking ones. The *hilarious* ones where it looks like both teams are trying to miss.

There was a time, not so long ago, when we genuinely believed we were **cursed from twelve yards**. It didn't matter who stepped up — Hirst, Brunt, Reach, your nan — if they wore blue and white and aimed at a spot, the ball was going wide, over, or straight at the keeper's knees.

We had shootouts where fans *refused* to watch. One bloke famously stood outside the ground chain-smoking through all five kicks. Another covered his eyes with a match programme from 1991 and shouted, "If this goes in, I'll never complain about Bovril again!"

The worst? Pick one.

- Losing to Wolves in the FA Cup after five perfect penalties — until we missed the sixth.
- That playoff semi in 2016 where the keeper danced on the line like a circus act and our lad scuffed it into orbit.

But then came 2023.

Peterborough. Second leg.

After the greatest comeback in Football League history, we still had to win it on penalties. Five nervous volunteers stepped forward. You could hear hearts beating in every corner of Hillsborough.

And one by one… they went in.

When Jack Hunt slotted the winner, Hillsborough **exploded**. Kids crying. Adults sprinting. Strangers collapsed in joy.
For once — *finally* — the penalty curse was broken.

Until next time, of course.

Because we're Wednesday.

And we never do anything the easy way.

CHAPTER 26: BLUE SANTA, INFLATABLE OWLS & FESTIVE MAYHEM

Christmas at Sheffield Wednesday isn't just tinsel and turkey — it's inflatable birds, lager-soaked carols, and one unforgettable bloke dressed as **Blue Santa**.

Every year, as December rolls in and the temperatures drop, the club transforms.
The Megastore fills with half-price mugs. The Kop starts chanting "Hi Ho Silver Lin-ing" to the tune of *Jingle Bells*. And fans arrive wearing more lights than Meadowhall.

But one year — **2014**, to be exact — things got *next level*.

Blue Santa arrived.

Nobody knows who started it. But halfway through a freezing game against Wigan, in the South Stand appeared a man in full Santa regalia — only it was blue and white from head to toe. Beard. Robe. Hat. Even his sack said *"Up The Owls."*

He handed out sweets. Took selfies. Sang *"We wish you a Wednesday Christmas."*

Then he lobbed an inflatable owl into the crowd.

Chaos.

Soon there were **dozens** of inflatable owls bouncing through the air. People booting them like beach balls. One landed on the pitch. The ref picked it up, looked confused, then chucked it back into the crowd. The Kop gave him a round of applause.

After we scored, Blue Santa ran up and down the aisle waving a flare like a rock star. Security tried to stop him, but the crowd started chanting *"Let him sleigh!"* and they backed off.

That year, we didn't win promotion. But we won the **spirit of**

football.

Because no matter where we are in the table, no matter how grim the weather or the ref, Wednesday fans turn up — with **madness, loyalty, and a touch of magic**.

Especially at Christmas.

CHAPTER 27: THE SHIRT THAT CHANGED EVERYTHING (AND STANK FOR WEEKS)

There's something sacred about a football shirt. It's not just cloth — it's **identity**. A badge of pride. A battle flag. And if you're a Wednesdayite, chances are you've got one shirt that tells *your* story.

Mine? 1995 home kit. Thick collar. Sanderson sponsor. Blue and white stripes like they'd been drawn with a felt-tip. It didn't fit right. Itched in summer. Froze in winter. And after one away day in Plymouth, it **absolutely stank**.

But I refused to wash it.

Because the first time I wore it, we *won* 3–0 away. Hirst scored a blinder. I spilled Bovril down the front. Didn't care. Wore it the next match — another win. Before I knew it, I was convinced the shirt was **magic**.

By Christmas, it could've walked on its own.

Mum tried to sneak it into the wash. I hid it under my bed. She said, "It smells like a bin fire." I said, "It smells like *victory*."

Over the years, that shirt went everywhere. Cup ties. Derbies. Dates (only once). It became a symbol — of belief, of madness, of blind faith in football superstition.

Ask any Wednesday fan and they'll have a shirt like that. One that's *far more than fabric*. One that still hangs in the cupboard, long after it stopped fitting.

Because it's not about how it looks. It's about what it **means**.

And mine? It means *Wednesday never dies* — even if the armpits might've tried to.

CHAPTER 28: FROM MEGASTORE TO MATCHDAY – WEIRDEST CLUB SHOP FINDS

Ah, the Sheffield Wednesday Megastore — part gift shop, part crypt of forgotten merchandise.

If you've ever wandered in before a match looking for a scarf and come out with an inflatable Darren Purse or a toaster that sings *Hi Ho Silver Lining*, then you know **exactly** what I'm talking about.

The club shop has been home to some of the finest and **strangest** bits of memorabilia ever to grace South Yorkshire.

Top finds include:

- The **1998 "Clappy Hands"** — blue plastic hands on a stick that made more noise than the West Stand on a wet Wednesday.
- The **Wednesday BBQ apron** — because what better way to flip burgers than with Reda Johnson across your chest?
- The **goalkeeper garden gnome** — genuinely terrifying, eyes like a haunted doll, but full kit accurate.
- The **ceramic owl with glow-in-the-dark eyes** — banned in some bedrooms after one fan reported "it watched me while I slept."

There was even a brief stint selling **club-branded lasagne**. No one knows why. Fewer know how it tasted.

But the best part? Watching tourists walk in and try to figure out what to buy. One confused American walked out with three air fresheners, a dog lead, and a copy of "Hillsborough: The Cookbook."

Still, we love it. Every mug, every mug-shaped alarm clock, every £2 keyring that stops working after a week. Because it's not just about shopping — it's about **supporting**, in the most wonderfully bonkers way possible.

Long live the Megastore.

And long live the **blue-and-white tat** we'll keep buying forever.

CHAPTER 29: OWLS ON TOUR – THE TIME WE GOT LOST IN LUTON

Luton away: a phrase whispered with dread and laughter in equal measure.

It was early 2005. League One slog. We were in the playoff chase, spirits were up, and hope was — as usual — dangerously high. So four of us, lifelong Wednesdayites, decided we'd do it *properly*: road trip, music, and service station snacks worthy of kings.

We had the gear.
Scarves. Shirts. An inflatable owl named Trevor. Even a thermos full of tea brewed so strong it could strip paint.

What we *didn't* have? A sense of direction.

The original plan was simple: straight down the M1, pull into Luton, park up, smash three points. Easy.

But then the sat-nav had an existential crisis. "Take the next exit," it said.
We ended up in **a garden centre outside Leicester**.

Then Milton Keynes, where we drove in circles around a concrete roundabout jungle, convinced we were being pranked by the local council. The straw that broke us was when we followed a diversion and ended up outside a **dentist's surgery** called "Smile United."

We weren't smiling.

We got to Luton an hour late. Kickoff already gone. We sprinted — literally sprinted — from a car park we weren't sure was legal, trying to find the stadium, which looked more like the back end of a 1980s housing estate.

Luton Town's Kenilworth Road? Let's be kind: it has *character*. The away entrance looked like someone's *front door*. We knocked. A bloke opened it and said, "Match started, lads. You're late."

We got in just in time to hear the cheer for **our goal** — the only one of the match. We'd missed it. We'd travelled 3½ hours and missed the very thing we came to see.

But here's the thing. The moment we hit the away end, scarves in the air, voices up, we remembered why we do it.

Because Wednesdayites aren't in it for convenience. We're in it for the chaos, the laughs, the shared struggle. That day, we didn't just support the club — we survived Luton. And in its own weird way, it was **perfect**.

Trevor the inflatable owl never made it back. He floated off during a celebratory chant and was last seen heading over a rooftop.

We still talk about him.
We still sing about that day.
And we still *never* trust that sat-nav again.

CHAPTER 30: THE DAY IT SNOWED INSIDE HILLSBOROUGH

You expect snow *around* Hillsborough. You don't expect it **on your lap in the middle of the South Stand**.

December 2010. Bristol Rovers at home. A dead rubber to most — unless you were a freezing, football-mad Wednesdayite looking for joy in the middle of a Yorkshire winter.

The game was forgettable. The **weather**, unforgettable.

By kickoff, flurries were already dusting the pitch. Fine. It's Yorkshire. But then, from nowhere, a swirling gust swept through the exposed sections of the stands and it started **snowing inside the stadium**. And not a light dusting. Proper flakes. Full-on winter wonderland vibes.

The Kop erupted in laughter, then in song:

> "It's snowing on the Wednesday! We're colder than the rest!"

A chant started comparing the referee's bald head to a snow globe. Someone made a snowman using a programme and a half-eaten sausage roll.
A small avalanche fell from the roof onto Row M. A lad stood up, arms wide, shouting, "I AM THE CHOSEN ONE!"

One steward tried to brush snow off the steps with a dustpan. Someone chucked a snowball at the away keeper.
Another started writing "UTTO" in the snow — short for "Up The..." well, you know the rest.

And the game? Sloppy. Slow. The ball skidded like a bar of soap. Their striker missed an open goal because his standing foot slid into Rotherham. One of ours tried a backheel and ended up doing a 720 spin on the spot.

We drew 1–1. Nobody remembered the goals. But **everyone** remembered the weather.

Because it wasn't just a match. It was a moment. The kind you get once a decade. The kind that becomes legend.

Even now, if snow starts falling before kickoff, someone will say, *"Remember that day against Bristol?"*
And if you were there, you'll smile, shiver, and nod.

Because only Wednesday can serve you a matchday experience that includes both Bovril **and blizzards** — in the same seat.

CHAPTER 31: 90 MINUTES OF RAIN, 90 MINUTES OF SINGING

Some matches are remembered for goals. Others, for drama.
This one? For **90 straight minutes of singing**... in **non-stop biblical rain**.

It was a midweek clash — mid-table, miserable, and soaking. I think it was against Huddersfield, or maybe Scunthorpe. Doesn't matter. The point is: nobody really turned up for the football. We turned up for each other.

The heavens opened at 6:45.
By 7:00, it was like a **monsoon had set up shop over Hillsborough**.

We were drenched before we reached the turnstiles. Scarves soaked. Trainers squelching. A bloke next to me had rain *inside his coat pockets*. Another used his pie as a sponge. Still ate it.

You'd think we'd moan. You'd think we'd groan.
But instead, we did what only Wednesdayites do — **we sang**.

It started as a bit of gallows humour — "Singing in the Rain" to the tune of *Hi Ho Silver Lining*.
Then "You Are My Wednesday" in full harmony.
Then someone bellowed: *"Who needs shelter when you've got passion!"*

The Kop responded with a roar.

For the full 90 minutes, we *didn't stop*. The match? Forgettable. Nil-nil. One shot on target. Both teams looked like they were running through porridge.

But in the stands? It was like **Woodstock with wet socks**.
A lad in Row H took his shirt off in protest at the ref's haircut. Another used a soaked matchday programme as a megaphone. And we chanted every classic we knew, inventing new ones on the

spot:

> "We're wetter than a Blades fan's eyes!"
> "Ref's so soaked, he's blowing bubbles!"
> "We're Wednesday, we're waterproof, and we're winning the noise!"

By the end, we were cold, soaked to the bone... and *buzzing*. It wasn't about the result. It was about the spirit. The unity. The mad joy of standing in a Yorkshire storm and *still refusing to be quiet*.

Because being a Wednesdayite means this:
When the rain falls hardest, **we sing louder**.

CHAPTER 32: THE PIE FELL OFF MY LAP – A LOVE STORY

They say you never forget your first love.
For me, it was steak and kidney — at Hillsborough — on a freezing February afternoon in 2003.

It was one of those days when everything feels like it's hanging by a thread. The game was tight. The crowd tense. The opposition (Oldham, I think) were playing the kind of negative football that made your teeth itch.

So I did what any Wednesdayite does to ease the nerves — I went to get a **pie**.

Hot. Fresh. Wrapped in paper that was already turning to mush from the steam. I clutched it like a newborn. Carried it back to my seat in the North Stand like it was gold. I sat. I balanced it on my lap. And just as I cracked open the lid... *it happened.*

A goal.
For us.

Crowd goes **mental**. Bodies flying. Seats rattling. I leap up, arms in the air, voice gone. And that pie — that sacred, steaming beauty — goes sailing.

It flies like a buttery UFO. Flips once. Twice. Then lands, face down, on the back of a stranger's head two rows down.

He turned. The pie slid off his coat. Silence.

I froze.
He looked at me... and *laughed.*
Then he chanted:

> "There's only one flying pie!"

The whole stand joined in. I got pats on the back. Someone handed me half a sausage roll in solidarity. We sang for the rest of the half. About the pie. About the goal. About Wednesday.

That's how it goes, isn't it?
You turn up for the football.
You stay for the chaos.
And you leave with a story.

It's not about results. It's about **moments** — messy, mental, magical ones — where a flying pie can bring strangers together better than any team talk.

And even now, I still say it:
That pie might've cost me £2.70… but it gave me a memory **worth a lifetime**.

CHAPTER 33: SINGING THROUGH SORROW – A TRIBUTE TO THE FANS WE LOST

Football gives us moments of joy — but it also gives us space to **grieve together**.

At Sheffield Wednesday, we've always done that with something bigger than silence: we do it with **song**.

Every season, we lose fans. Grandads who stood on the Kop since the 1950s. Dads who passed on their season ticket like a birthright. Best mates who never missed a game.
And when they go, we don't forget.
We remember them — **loudly**.

You'll be at Hillsborough, mid-match, tension building, and suddenly a chant starts:

"There's only one... [insert name here]!"

It echoes. It grows. And in that moment, you feel it — the presence of someone **who should still be here**. Someone whose voice helped shape this club's songbook.

I remember one game in 2016, we lost a fan called Terry — a Wednesday nutter who used to paint his face blue and dance like Bez in the North Stand. His mates brought a huge flag with his name on it. At the 67th minute — his age — the whole stand stood up and sang:

"Terry, Terry, give us a wave!"

People wept. Grown adults, arm in arm.
Because in Wednesday world, you don't vanish when you go. You become **part of the fabric**.

Some of our best moments have been shared with those who aren't here anymore — and you better believe they were still watching from somewhere.

Whether it's the "minute's applause," a scarf laid on a seat, or just a whispered toast in The Riverside pre-match…
We carry every one of them with us.
In chants.
In memories.
In **the roar after a goal**, when we all look up for just a second longer.

Because Wednesday isn't just a club. It's a family — one that **never stops singing for its own**.

CHAPTER 34: BALL BOYS, BANTER & THAT TIME ONE SCORED

If you want real chaos, don't look at the players. Look at the **ball boys**.

Every club's got them, but at Wednesday, our ball boys have always had a bit of a *spark*. More than once, they've been the difference between a snoozefest and a legendary tale.

There was the time a lad near the dugouts started **throwing the ball like Rory Delap**, launching it so far he got a round of applause. Another match, one hid the match ball under his hoodie during a time-wasting masterclass — got a wink from the gaffer and a ban from ball duty for a month.

But the best story?
The day a ball boy **scored**.

It was a pre-season friendly, quiet day, maybe 7,000 in the ground. A player's shot bobbled wide, slowly rolling toward the South Stand corner. Before anyone could react, this ball boy — probably no older than 12 — sprinted after it, wound up, and **smashed it back onto the pitch**.

Thing is... he hit it *perfectly*.

It looped over the keeper, bounced, and landed in the net. **Top corner. Absolute beauty.**

The crowd **erupted**.

He raised his arms like Shearer. Security tried to drag him off. The ref didn't know whether to laugh or book him. The announcer came over the tannoy:

"And it's 1–0 to the ball boys!"

That kid became a legend overnight. Got interviewed by Radio

Sheffield. Offered a spot in the academy. He turned it down — said he preferred PE with his mates and pork pies at halftime.

To this day, people swear he could've gone pro.

But the point is this: at Wednesday, **you don't need to wear the shirt to become a hero**. You just need to *show up, love it, and go for it* — whether you're in Row Z or chasing a stray ball near the touchline.

And if your name ends up in the fanzine next week? Even better.

CHAPTER 35: WEDNESDAY WEDDINGS, TATTOOS & BLUE BABIES

Being a Wednesdayite isn't a phase — it's a **lifestyle**, a **blood type**, and sometimes… **a wedding theme**.

We've all seen it. A bride walking down the aisle in a white dress with a blue sash. The groom waiting at the front, tie patterned like the 1991 home kit. The best man sneaking a matchday programme into his speech.

And let's be honest — no wedding is truly complete without someone chanting *"You are my Wednesday…"* during the buffet queue.

I once went to a do in Hillsborough's hospitality suite. The couple said their vows **underneath a giant framed photo of David Hirst**. Their first dance was to *Hi Ho Silver Lining*. The cake? Blue-and-white tiers with a fondant owl on top. Aunty Jean tried to eat it thinking it was chocolate. It was polystyrene.

Then there are the **tattoos**.

Wednesday fans don't do things by halves. We've got club badges on calves. Hillsborough's postcode across shoulders. Even "SWFC 4 LIFE" across knuckles. I met a bloke in Majorca who'd had Carlton Palmer inked on his back — full kit, full stretch. Said he lost a bet in 1992. Still wears it with pride.

And of course… there's the **blue babies**.

We've seen 'em. Brand-new humans wrapped in miniature Wednesday kits before they've even opened their eyes. Tiny booties. "Born Owl" bibs. One lad even had his name registered as **Wensday** — no joke. His mum said it "felt right."

Because when you support this club, you don't just follow it. You *build your life around it*. From the aisle to the tattoo chair to the maternity ward, Wednesday isn't just with you — it *is* you. And long may it continue.

CHAPTER 36: RIVALRY RELOADED – BEATING LEEDS WITH 10 MEN

No fixture fires the blood quite like a Yorkshire derby.
But when it's **Leeds**… it hits *different*.

Forget the niceties. The handshake before kickoff. The polite "respect" in the stands. This one? This is war painted in blue and white, fought in the mud and under the lights.

One match in particular still echoes like a war drum — Wednesday vs Leeds, 2007.
We were struggling. They were smug. Their fans turned up like royalty. They left like peasants.

Midway through the first half, we went down to **10 men**. Dubious red. Ref had a Yorkshire accent, but he might've been from *Mars* the way he saw it.

They laughed. Sang songs. Gave it the big one.
They shouldn't have.

Because what followed was **pure, unfiltered defiance**.

We dug in. We fought for every blade of grass. And with fifteen minutes left, we broke on the counter. A chipped cross. A diving header. **GOAL.**

The ground **erupted**. People falling over rows. Pints flying. A bloke next to me screamed "I LOVE THIS CLUB" and kissed a stranger's dog.

And then — the magic.

Final whistle.
1–0. Ten men. Leeds flattened.
And the chant roared out from the Kop like thunder from the gods:

> *"We only need ten, we only need ten…"*

The Leeds fans, silenced, shuffled out like ghosts.

We'd beaten them with guts, heart, and one less man — and it tasted better than any cup final win.

Because at Wednesday, it's not just about football. It's about **pride**. About sticking two fingers up to anyone who doubts us.

Especially *them*.

CHAPTER 37: MATCHDAY SUPERSTITIONS – LUCKY SOCKS AND WEIRD ROUTINES

Being a Wednesdayite means **hoping** for the best. But sometimes hope alone doesn't cut it.

So what do we do?

We build shrines. We whisper to pint glasses. We wear the *same pair of socks* every matchday — unwashed, sacred, mildly terrifying.

Superstition, my friends, runs deep in S6.

I know a bloke who's worn the same faded home shirt since 1999 — only for home games. He once turned around on the motorway because he realised he'd packed the away kit by mistake. Missed kickoff. Still said it was "worth it for the points."

Another lad eats exactly three bacon sandwiches before every Saturday game. Not one. Not two. **Three.** He calls them "the holy trinity" — bread, pig, and promotion dreams.

Then there's Big Linda from the Kop, who brings a plastic owl named Trevor to every home game. Rubs its beak before kickoff. We went on a seven-match unbeaten run with Trevor in attendance. When she forgot it once? We lost 4–0. Coincidence? She doesn't think so. Neither do we.

Some rituals get stranger:

- One fan only walks up the *left* side of the Leppings Lane steps.
- Another has to hear the *theme from Gladiators* before leaving the house.
- A couple in Rotherham reportedly watch the pre-match warm-up in silence, holding hands, facing Hillsborough from their back garden — even if they're not going to the

game.

And let's not even start on the **lucky pants**.

But here's the truth: when you support Wednesday, you cling to *anything* that feels like control.
Because the results might not be in our hands — but our rituals, our socks, our sacred pre-match Greggs order... **those are ours**.

And if we win? You better believe we're doing the exact same thing next week.

CHAPTER 38: WHEN WE TOOK OVER BLACKPOOL

Away days are always special. But sometimes... they become **legend**.

Blackpool, 2011. Final day of the season. Glorious sunshine. Nothing much at stake, but *thousands* of Wednesdayites turned up like it was the Champions League Final.

It was supposed to be a normal weekend. It turned into **Sheffield-by-the-Sea**.

The promenade? Covered in blue and white. Flags hung from hotel balconies. Deckchairs replaced by singing fans. Pints flowing by 10 a.m. Someone built a sand sculpture of Hillsborough. One lad wore a full owl costume and crowd-surfed in the sea.

You couldn't walk two steps without hearing *"We are Wednesday..."* or *"You Fill Up My Senses"* belted out with sunburnt passion.

By 2 p.m., every pub had run out of lager. A landlady at one boozer just shrugged and said, "We didn't know you were all mental."

The game itself? Irrelevant. We drew 1–1. No one cared.
Because **the day was ours**.

There was a conga line of Wednesdayites dancing through the Pleasure Beach. A bloke got a Wednesday badge shaved into his back hair on the pier. We turned karaoke night into a live rendition of every terrace chant from 1983 onwards.

And the beach? Full of beer cans, inflatable owls, and *pride*.

It wasn't about promotion. It wasn't about revenge.
It was about **joy**, community, and proving that we are — without doubt — the **loudest, proudest, daftest set of fans in the country**.

MARTYN LEARY

Blackpool never stood a chance.

They called the police — but the only thing we were guilty of was **loving this club too loudly**.

CHAPTER 39: OWLS QUOTES AND SAYINGS – THE GOSPEL ACCORDING TO HILLSBOROUGH

Some clubs have slogans.
Wednesday has **scripture**.

From the terraces to the turnstiles, our language is its own dialect — part poetry, part pub talk, part pure northern magic. If you've ever stood shoulder-to-shoulder on the Kop or argued about team sheets at the pub, you've heard the sayings that stitch us together.

They're not just quotes. They're **truths** — passed down like family recipes and told with the sort of conviction usually reserved for religious sermons or chip shop orders.

Here are just a few of the greatest hits:

> **"We are Wednesday, aren't we?"**
> It's not a question. It's a statement. A philosophy. A reminder that no matter what the world throws at us — relegation, referees, rainstorms — we belong to something bigger. Something we didn't choose, but were chosen by.

> **"I was born Wednesday, and I'll die Wednesday."**
> You'll hear this shouted from the back of buses or whispered after a defeat. It means loyalty. It means sticking by the club when it's 5–0 down and still singing.

> **"We never do it easy."**
> Fact. Whether it's a penalty shootout, a last-minute promotion chase, or turning up to beat Man Utd after losing to Port Vale — Wednesdayites know that drama is part of the DNA.

> **"We're massive, aren't we?"**
> Said with a wink. Said with pride. Said whether we're top

of the league or 17th in League One. "Massive" isn't about trophies — it's about *us*.

"Up the Owls."
Simple. Universal. The greeting, the parting words, the call to arms. It's tattooed, spray-painted, shouted across motorways and whispered into scarves on cold December nights.

These sayings are more than catchphrases. They're our **inheritance**.

They link strangers in away ends. They start chants, end arguments, and fill silences with belonging.

They're how you know someone else *gets it*.

And when words fail — in joy or heartbreak — they're what we fall back on.

Because when you wear blue and white, every phrase becomes part of your identity.

And when someone shouts, "You Owls?" — you never hesitate.

"Too right, pal. All my life."

CHAPTER 40: DREAM WEDNESDAY XI AND CLOSING WORDS – ONCE AN OWL, ALWAYS AN OWL

Every Wednesdayite, at some point, has had this debate: **Who makes your all-time XI?**

The greatest players. The hardest tacklers. The trickiest wingers. The cult heroes. The fan favourites. The "you-had-to-be-there" legends.

Here's mine — and yes, I'll defend it in the pub with my life:

GK: Kevin Pressman

Fat bloke's reflexes. Brick wall with a side of chips.

Defence:

- **RB: Roland Nilsson** – Rolls-Royce of a player. Could glide past traffic.
- **CB: Des Walker** – Didn't need to tackle because no one could catch him.
- **CB: Reda Johnson** – Scored headers, broke bones (mainly his own), smiled through it all.
- **LB: Nigel Worthington** – Steady as a pint on a level table.

Midfield:

- **RM: Chris Waddle** – Genius with a mullet. Could beat a man with one eyebrow raise.
- **CM: John Sheridan** – Shinner king. Controlled games while looking like he'd rather be in a pub.
- **CM: Barry Bannan** – Current wizard. See the pass? He *invented* it.
- **LM: Chris Brunt** – Left foot like Thor's hammer. Could cross a ball from Ecclesall Road.

☐ **Strikers:**
- **ST: David Hirst** – Built like a house, ran like a horse, hit like a hammer.
- **ST: Jermaine Johnson** – Madness in motion. Never knew what he'd do. Neither did he.

Manager? Big Ron. For the coat, the chaos, the cigar.

But really, we all have our own dream team — not just the players, but the people **we watched with**.

Your dad in the South Stand. Your mate who knew the songs before you could talk. The stranger who hugged you after Windass' header.

Because that's the thing. This book? These stories? These chapters?

They're not really about the players. They're about **us**.

The ones who stood in the rain. Who screamed at 90+5. Who cried at relegation and still bought a season ticket the next day.

We've sung through sorrow. Laughed through heartbreak. Danced through disaster.

And we'll keep doing it.

Because there's one thing no defeat, no dodgy ref, no relegation can ever take away:

We are all Wednesday, aren't we?

Forever.

Up the Owls.

☐ **Bonus Chapters**

41. The Day We All Turned Into Managers
From screaming tactics at the telly to drawing 4-4-2s on beermats

— a tribute to the armchair gaffers of Sheffield.

42. The Bovril That Burnt My Soul (And I'd Do It Again)
Scalded tongue, frozen hands — but somehow still the best drink in the world on a matchday.

43. DIY Scarves, Homemade Flags & Duvet Covers as Banners
How Wednesdayites turn whatever they can find into blue-and-white gold.

44. The Wednesday That Got Me Through Divorce, Redundancy & Everything Else
A personal tribute to how the club holds us together when everything else falls apart.

45. Pub Tales and Pre-Match Lies
The legendary nonsense told over pints before kickoff — from "we're definitely signing Ronaldo" to "I once nutmegged John Harkes in Lidl."

46. How to Spot a Wednesdayite Anywhere in the World
Blue wristband? Accent? That look in the eye when you say "Hillsborough"? We're everywhere — and we know our own.

47. The Worst Kits We Ever Loved
Pink and grey horror shows. Stripe misfires. We wore them anyway — and we still do.

48. Wednesday in Film, Music & Tattoos on Strange Body Parts
Where we've spotted the Owls unexpectedly — including one fan's *Chris Brunt tattoo on his thigh.*

49. Honking Horns, Open Bus Windows & The Promotion Parade That Took 6 Hours
Celebrating like lunatics — even when we came second. Especially then.

50. What Wednesday Means to Me – Fan Voices from Around the World
Messages from real supporters. Scotland to Singapore. Barnsley to

Bangkok. The badge means the same everywhere.

Bonus Chapter 41: The Day We All Turned Into Managers

Every Wednesdayite has, at some point, transformed into **Carlos Carvalhal in the kitchen**, or Big Ron in the beer garden.

We all do it — second guess the lineup, critique the subs, and scream "Why is he bringing him on!?" like we've got a UEFA Pro Licence and a tactics board in the shed.

You'll hear it everywhere:

- *"Three at the back? What's he thinking?"*
- *"Play two up top, always. Doesn't matter who."*
- *"I'd have subbed him at half-time, but what do I know?"*

One bloke I know brings a notebook to matches. Writes down the shape. Tracks possession. Calls it "The Wednesday Tactical Log." He's been doing it since 2008. Hasn't changed his opinion once. Every game? *"We need a midfield general and a big lad up front."*

We argue on WhatsApp, on Twitter, on bar stools with crisps as tactics pieces. We're *all* gaffers when we win — and even better ones when we lose.

Because deep down, that's what makes this club special: it doesn't just belong to the players. It belongs to **us**, too.

Even if none of us could survive 10 minutes in the actual dugout.

Bonus Chapter 42: The Bovril That Burnt My Soul (And I'd Do It Again)

It's cold. It's wet. The match is duller than a midweek maths class.

What saves you?

Bovril.

That salty, lava-hot, beefy brown elixir handed over in a paper cup that collapses slightly as you take it. One sip and your tongue **melts**, your eyebrows sweat, and somehow — you feel better.

I've spilt it on myself. Burnt my gums. Choked mid-cheer. Still — I wouldn't swap it for a hot chocolate in a fancy café if you paid me.

There's something spiritual about sipping Bovril while watching a team try to break down Cheltenham Town in a snowstorm.

It's not just a drink. It's **matchday medicine**.

My mate once brought his own flask because he said the turnstile Bovril wasn't "beefy enough." He ended up pouring it out for a stranger when we scored a 94th-minute winner. That moment? Pure magic.

Burnt lips. Frozen fingers. Glory.

That's **Wednesday Bovril**.

Bonus Chapter 43: DIY Scarves, Homemade Flags & Duvet Covers as Banners

Wednesdayites don't just buy their gear — we **create** it.

Scarves knitted by aunties, flags painted in back gardens, and one particularly mad genius who once brought a **bed sheet with "Up The Owls" spray-painted across it in luminous paint**. It glowed in the away end. Glowed.

We've seen duvet covers repurposed into banners. One lad even turned his mum's old curtains into a cape for the 2016 playoff final.

Felt-tip signs on cereal boxes. Tinfoil FA Cups. Scarves knitted in dodgy stripes that somehow became *lucky*. Even when the badge is upside down, if it's homemade — it's **perfect**.

Why?

Because it's not about branding. It's about **belonging**.

Every flag is a love letter. Every scarf is a song.

And every kid who colours "SWFC" on a bit of cardboard and waves it at the telly? That's a new generation, writing their own chapter.

Bonus Chapter 44: The Wednesday That Got Me Through Divorce, Redundancy & Everything Else

We talk about football like it's just a game.

But for many of us — it's a **lifeline**.

I've seen it first-hand. Mates who went through break-ups, bereavements, lost jobs... but still turned up at Hillsborough. Still stood on the terrace. Still sang.

Because when everything else falls apart, Wednesday is **always there**.

It doesn't ask questions. It doesn't care how rough the week's been. It gives you 90 minutes where the outside world fades. Just you, your scarf, and eleven lads trying their best (sometimes badly).

It gives you *structure*.
Routine.
Hope.

Even in the darkest seasons, this club gives us **light**.

And sometimes, all it takes is one chant, one goal, one hug from a stranger in Row J — and suddenly, things don't feel so heavy.

Because this isn't just a football club.

It's **home**.

Bonus Chapter 45: Pub Tales and Pre-Match Lies

Ah, the pub before kickoff — the real **press conference**.

It's where transfer rumours are born and truth dies a slow death in a pint of lager.

> "My cousin's mate's dad saw Kieran Lee at Asda. Said he's signing again."
> "We're buying a Croatian left-back. Speaks four languages. Two of them fluent."
> "The gaffer's dropped half the team. Heard it from the cleaner at Middlewood Road."

Nonsense. All of it. And we lap it up like gospel.

Then there's the exaggeration:

> "I once nutmegged Chris Waddle in a car park."
> "Hirsty gave me a tenner once and said 'keep believing.'"
> "I'm banned from six away grounds for singing too loud."

Even the match predictions:

> "4–0, easy. This new lad's like Messi with sideburns."

We know it's lies.
We *love* that it's lies.

Because the pub before the game isn't about truth. It's about **hope**. Banter. Brotherhood. Belief.

And if half of it ends up on the group chat under "Utter Nonsense"? Even better.

Bonus Chapter 46: How to Spot a Wednesdayite Anywhere in the World

You can spot us from a mile off. Doesn't matter if you're in Sheffield or **Singapore** — Wednesdayites give off a certain... *vibe*.

Clues:

- A blue-and-white wristband at a wedding.
- A tattoo of an owl peeking out of a shirt sleeve.

- That look in the eye when someone says, "You football?"

Say "*Wednesday*" and watch them **light up**.

I once met a bloke in Tenerife wearing a black t-shirt with a tiny SWFC badge sewn on by his nan. We spent the next hour chanting "We are Wednesday" in a beach bar while confused Germans clapped along.

From Australia to Alicante, we turn up.

We don't just follow a team. We **carry it with us**.

On flags. On hats. In hearts.

And when you meet a fellow Owl abroad? It's not just a meeting — it's a **reunion**.

Bonus Chapter 47: The Worst Kits We Ever Loved

Some kits are **masterpieces**.

Others? Crimes against eyesight.

Yet somehow — we **loved them anyway**.

- The 1993 grey and pink away kit? Looked like a bruised pigeon. Iconic.
- That weird chevron thing from the early 2000s? Confused everyone. Still sold out.
- The pinstripe one with the sponsor that peeled off in the rain? Legendary.

We mocked them. We bought them. We wore them until they fell apart.

Because kits aren't just shirts. They're **memories**.

We remember who we were dating. What song was on the radio. Where we stood in the ground.

Even the worst ones — especially the worst ones — become beloved. Part of the journey.

If you see someone wearing that luminous yellow third kit from 1997?

Respect them. They've seen things.

Bonus Chapter 48: Wednesday in Film, Music & Tattoos on Strange Body Parts

We pop up everywhere.

Blink and you'll spot an SWFC sticker in a music video. A Hillsborough reference in a gritty BBC drama. A guitar strap with stripes in a pub gig in Rotherham.

Our influence sneaks in like a cheeky backheel.

Even the **tattoos** have taken on legendary status.

I've seen:

- "Up the Owls" on the inside of a lip.
- A stylised David Hirst on a shoulder blade.
- One brave soul with Chris Brunt's face on their thigh… with angel wings.

We don't do things by halves.

We *declare our love* — loudly, proudly, and often permanently.

Because whether it's on screen, on stage, or on skin…
Wednesday follows us everywhere.

Bonus Chapter 49: Honking Horns, Open Bus Windows & The Promotion Parade That Took 6 Hours

When we go up — we don't just celebrate. We **invade** joy.

There's nothing like a Wednesday promotion parade.

The city turns blue. Flags hang from bedroom windows. Horns honk. Cars are overloaded with scarf-waving lunatics yelling,

"We're massive!" into the wind.

The 2005 parade? Took **six hours** to crawl from the stadium to the town centre. One bus got stuck outside a Greggs. Fans didn't care — sang on the roof. A guy handed a sausage roll to Lee Bullen out of a second-storey window.

People danced on bins. Babies waved flags. Grandmas cried.

You don't forget those days.

Because we don't just celebrate success — we **explode** with it.

Bonus Chapter 50: What Wednesday Means to Me – Fan Voices from Around the World

It's more than a club. More than a badge.

It's **identity. Memory. Belonging.**

I asked Wednesdayites everywhere what the club means to them.

Here's what they said:

> "It's my dad's voice in my head every Saturday." – *Dave, Canada*
> "It's how I make friends in pubs in countries I can't spell." – *Liam, Thailand*
> "It's the only place I've ever felt truly home." – *Sarah, Norfolk*
> "It's heartbreak, comedy, chaos — and I wouldn't swap it for anything." – *Sam, Sheffield*

We're scattered across the globe, but connected by one thing:

Wednesday.

We carry it with us. In our chants, our memories, our hearts.

Once an Owl…

Always.

🗨 BONUS SECTION: THE BLADES BANTER – DERBY DAYS THAT DEFINED US

51. The History: 131 Battles, One Divided City
A stats-packed look at every major milestone in the Steel City rivalry — wins, losses, draws, red cards, and more.

52. Boxing Day Massacre Revisited – 4–0 and Still Glorious
A full breakdown of *that* 1979 game — who scored, what was said, and why they've never got over it.

53. When the Ref Was Red and So Were We
A collection of the worst (and funniest) refereeing decisions in derby history — and how we reacted like only Wednesdayites can.

54. Blades in Disguise – The Wednesday Players They Tried to Steal
A look at players who crossed the divide, nearly did, or flat-out refused to — with tales of betrayal and blue-and-white loyalty.

55. The Best Wednesday Goals vs United (Ranked by Cheek & Chaos)
From thunderbolts to tap-ins, a definitive top 10 of the best derby goals ever scored in blue and white.

56. Red Cards, Rain Delays & Riot Vans – The Wildest Derby Days
The most explosive, unhinged matches — with flying elbows, lost pies, and one very confused ball boy.

57. Heroes of the Hillsborough Half – Our Derby Day Legends
Profiles of players who owned the derby: Waddle, Hirst, Curran, Windass, and a few surprise cult icons.

58. "Mind the Gap!" and Other Famous Chants That Drove Them Mad
A look at the chants, banners, and songs that wound them up more than a soft penalty in injury time.

59. The One Where They Thought They Had Us
Games where the Blades thought it was all over — and we came back to break their hearts in glorious fashion.

60. It's More Than Football – Why the Derby Really Matters
A deep dive into what this rivalry says about the city, the fans, and why **Wednesday will always be the bigger club** (with evidence, of course).

CHAPTER 51: THE HISTORY – 131 BATTLES, ONE DIVIDED CITY

There are rivalries… and then there's **Sheffield Wednesday vs Sheffield United**.

Not built on fake drama or Premier League hype, this one was born in **industry**, raised on **bitterness**, and fuelled by generations who'd rather lose a cup final than lose *this* fixture.

It's not just football. It's **religion**.
Blue vs Red. Steel vs Steel. One city — two clubs who've been at each other's throats since 1890.

 Key Stats (as of 2024):

- **131 total competitive meetings**
- **Wednesday wins:** 42
- **Draws:** 43
- **United wins:** 46
- **Most goals in a single game:** 7 (Wednesday 4–3 Blades, 1991)
- **Biggest win:** Wednesday 4–0 United (Boxing Day, 1979)
- **Most red cards in one game:** 3 — and we still finished with more dignity.

But stats only tell part of the story. The real magic is in the moments — and the *madness*.

The time a fan ran on and kissed the corner flag after we equalised in the 94th. The lad who proposed on the Kop after a 2–1 win and got a "YES" in front of 30,000. The time a Blades fan left at halftime and came back dressed in blue to celebrate a Wednesday comeback.

No other derby is this real. This rooted.

These games split families. Decide marriages. Wreck birthdays. Fuel pubs for *decades*. Kids grow up picking sides by which scarf made them cry more — and never, ever switch.

When Wednesday win, the city *sings*.
When United win, the city sulks.
But when it's a draw? Nobody speaks to each other for days.

This rivalry is Sheffield.
And in Sheffield, **Wednesday will always be the real heartbeat**.

CHAPTER 52: BOXING DAY MASSACRE REVISITED – 4–0 AND STILL GLORIOUS

Some days become folklore. Others become **war cries**.
Boxing Day 1979 became **both**.

It wasn't just a game. It was a **demolition** — the day Sheffield Wednesday ripped apart their red-and-white neighbours like a Christmas cracker with dynamite inside.

The build-up was classic derby stuff.
United were higher in the league. Confident. Smug. Their fans turned up in numbers, expecting an easy three points.

But they weren't ready for what was coming.
Because that day, we didn't just beat them.
We **destroyed them**.

 Final Score:

Wednesday 4 – 0 United

- **Goals:**
    - Terry Curran (1)
    - Ian Mellor (1)
    - Jeff King (2)
- **Attendance:** Over 49,000 packed into Hillsborough
- **Atmosphere:** Nuclear

Terry Curran ran rings around them. Mellor's finish had style. But it was Jeff King who delivered the final two daggers — one a thunderous finish, the other a slide-in that sent the Kop into orbit.

The Blades? Shellshocked. Some of them walked out by the third goal. Others stayed just to suffer.

We sang them out of the stadium. Loud. Relentless.

> "Four–nil on your special day…"

"Can we play you every week?"
"Merry Christmas, United!"

Aftermath:

United's manager said it was "embarrassing."
One of their defenders said it was "like a dream gone wrong."
For us? It was a **fever dream of joy** we've never quite woken up from.

Even now, decades later, they *still* can't talk about it without wincing. And we *still* chant about it every derby. Because this wasn't just a win — it was a **turning point in the power of the city**.

Every Wednesday fan born after 1979 knows the story like scripture.

"Where were you on Boxing Day?"

If you say **Hillsborough**, heads nod. Smiles grow.
And someone whispers:

"Best Christmas I ever had."

CHAPTER 53: WHEN THE REF WAS RED AND SO WERE WE

If you want to see a stadium **collectively combust**, just watch a referee butcher a decision in a Steel City derby.

Because in Sheffield, **bad refereeing doesn't just get booed** — it becomes *legend*.

Derby matches are never calm. Never tidy. But throw in a referee with a whistle addiction or eyes painted on, and you've got a recipe for pure carnage.

Let's go through a few of the classics.

☐ 1993 – The Phantom Penalty

Hillsborough. Tight game. Wednesday in control. Ball bounces in our box. Their striker dives like he's been shot by a sniper on the roof.

Ref points to the spot.

Even the *United* fans looked confused. The crowd? Incandescent. One bloke next to me launched his meat and potato pie into orbit. Missed the goal. Missed the player. Hit the assistant referee right in the back of the head.

They scored. Match finished 1–1. Crowd still singing "One-eyed ref!" all the way to the tram.

☐ 2002 – 13 Yellow Cards, 2 Reds, 0 Control

This one turned into a war zone.
Blades flying into tackles like it was Mortal Kombat. We responded in kind.

The ref? He started handing out cards like it was Christmas in

Card Factory.

At one point, both managers were yelling at him in *unison*.
A pitch invader tried to offer him a pair of glasses. He got banned for life. The glasses were **prescription**.

☐ The Derby Where He Forgot the Rules (Yes, Really)

Mid-90s. Ball went out for a throw. He gave a corner.
We all screamed. He looked panicked, turned to his assistant… who shrugged.
He stuck with the corner. They scored.
After the match, he claimed "it was windy." It wasn't. Not even a breeze. The man was guessing.

☐ Honorable Mentions:

- The red card for "aggressive eye contact" (actual quote).
- The offside given against a throw-in.
- The booking for time-wasting… in the *5th minute*.

In Sheffield derbies, **bad refs become part of the fabric.**

We chant about them. We write fanzine articles. We name our dogs after them (as an insult).

And every time they mess it up?

We grow **louder**.

Because while refs come and go, Wednesday pride never misses a decision.

CHAPTER 54: BLADES IN DISGUISE – THE WEDNESDAY PLAYERS THEY TRIED TO STEAL

There's loyalty.
There's rivalry.
And then there's **refusing to go to the red side of Sheffield — even for a pay rise**.

We've had players who've made their names on our side of the Steel City divide — and stayed **true**. But we've also had whispers. Rumours. Nearlys. And the **few brave souls** who crossed over and lived to tell the tale (barely).

Let's break it down.

▢ The Ones They Wanted (But Never Got)

David Hirst
In the mid-90s, there were rumblings United wanted to bring Hirsty in during an injury spell.
The rumour lasted 12 hours. Hirsty laughed it off. Said he'd "rather retire than wear red."
We believed him. He stayed. He scored. He *became legend*.

Barry Bannan
Yes, they've tried. More than once.
But Baz is Hillsborough through and through.
He's the beating heart of the modern side — and once said in an interview:

> *"The only red I'd ever wear is a Santa hat at training."*

Icon.

Chris Waddle
They couldn't afford his hairspray, never mind his feet.

🔵 The Ones Who Crossed the Line

Leigh Bromby
Played for both. Said all the right things. But deep down, we knew where his loyalty really landed — he once celebrated a Wednesday goal louder than the crowd.

Alan Quinn
A decent player. Came through our academy. Then put on red.
We sang about him for years — none of it printable.

🧊 The Ice-Cold Refusals

Terry Curran
They sniffed around. He growled and said something so Yorkshire the agent backed off.

Lee Bullen
Captain. Legend. Tried, tested, true.
United could've offered him the moon and he'd still say:

> "No thanks, I'm Owls 'til I die."

In Sheffield, **crossing sides isn't just about transfers**.
It's about **identity**.
And while some chose the red… the ones who stayed blue?

They became icons.

Because there's loyalty —
And then there's **Wednesday loyalty**.

CHAPTER 55: THE BEST WEDNESDAY GOALS VS UNITED (RANKED BY CHEEK & CHAOS)

Some goals win games.
Others win arguments for **decades**.

And in Sheffield, there's no sweeter goal than one scored against *them*. Whether it's a screamer, a tap-in, or a flukey deflection off someone's backside — if it hits the red net, it goes in the **hall of fame**.

Here are our **top Wednesday goals against United**, ranked not just by beauty — but by **sh*thousery, timing, and sheer chaos**.

☐ Chris Waddle (FA Cup Semi-Final, 1993)

Wembley. The world watching.
Waddle picks it up. One shimmy, one strike, and the ball bends into the corner like it's been remote controlled.
Cue **Barry Davies' immortal line**:

> "You have to say, that's magnificent!"
> Still gives goosebumps. A masterpiece. A derby goal for the ages.

☐ Josh Windass (2020)

Let's be honest: we were struggling. Morale was low.
Then Windass turned up with a bullet strike that nearly took the net off at the Lane.
Shushed their fans. Celebrated like a man who'd just avenged generations.
He got it.
We got it.
They hated it.

Terry Curran (Boxing Day Massacre, 1979)

Started it all. Ran at their back line like a man on a mission, buried it with venom.
The roar was deafening. Set the tone for a **4–0 slaughter** that lives on in pub debates and bedtime stories.

Honourable Mentions:

- **Jermaine Johnson (2011)** – Ran the length of the pitch like Sonic on Red Bull and slotted it past a keeper who's still having nightmares.
- **Marcus Tudgay (2009)** – Nutmegged their defender, curled one in like a Christmas bow, and cupped his ear with absolute **violence**.
- **David Hirst (1991)** – Left foot. Top bins. Net still shaking.

Whether it's at Hillsborough, Bramall Lane, or a neutral ground that gets torn in half, these goals matter more than most.

They don't just win games.

They win **bragging rights forever**.

CHAPTER 56: RED CARDS, RAIN DELAYS & RIOT VANS – THE WILDEST DERBY DAYS

Steel City derbies are **not normal**.

They're not "football matches." They're full-blown festivals of chaos, tears, weather tantrums, questionable officiating, and more **red cards than a Valentine's Day party in prison**.

Here's a rundown of the **wildest, most ridiculous derby days** where everything went off the rails — and we absolutely loved it.

☐ 2001 – The "Let's Just Send Everyone Off" Match

- 2 red cards
- 11 yellows
- One assistant ref got **accidentally tackled** by a player
- The ball ended up in the crowd so often it could've applied for a season ticket

Players were sliding into tackles like they were trying to enter another postcode.
Fans were so loud the ref apparently asked for earplugs at half-time.

We drew. But it felt like a **boxing match with extra pies**.

☐ 1997 – Rain Delay Derby

Started like any other game… until **biblical rain** came down in the 18th minute.

Fans huddled under flags. A bloke tried to sell bin bags for £2 each. The lines got washed off the pitch.

We were sure it would be abandoned — until the groundsman turned up with *a mop and a dream*. Ten minutes later, we were back on.

We won 2–1.
Still reckon the ref's decision to continue was divine intervention.

☐ 2002 – Riot Van Row

Tensions so high the police turned up early — and stayed.

One fan got escorted out for waving a **blow-up owl** in a provocative manner.
A pensioner in the South Stand started a chant so offensive it ended up on local news.
After full time, both sets of fans tried to out-sing each other from either side of a KFC. No arrests. Just sore throats.

☐ The Ball Boy Incident

In the mid-2000s, a ball boy at Hillsborough accidentally nutmegged a United player with a stray pass. Crowd **erupted**. Player tried to square up to him. Ball boy got subbed off by the fourth official for "safety reasons."

He returned the next week to a standing ovation.

In the Steel City, chaos isn't the exception — it's the **expectation**.

And the wilder it gets?

The more we remember it.

Because this rivalry isn't neat, clean, or quiet. It's **mad**, messy, and beautiful.

Just the way we like it.

CHAPTER 57: HEROES OF THE HILLSBOROUGH HALF – OUR DERBY DAY LEGENDS

Some players just **get it**.

They don't need a history lesson or a pep talk about Sheffield's split loyalty — they step onto that pitch on derby day and play like the badge is stitched into their chest.

These are the **Owls legends** who made derby days their playgrounds. Some were stars. Some were unexpected. All of them are **heroes**.

☐ Chris Waddle

A baller for the big occasion. That goal in the '93 semi-final wasn't just class — it was **definitive**.
Glided through red shirts like they were cones. Wembley stage. National spotlight.
Sheffield's war, *his* orchestra.

☐ Terry Curran

Scorer in the **Boxing Day Massacre**.
Played like a man possessed. Blew kisses to the crowd after scoring. Mocked the Blades in post-match interviews.
He wasn't just a player — he was a **showman**, and they hated every second of it.

☐ Josh Windass

Modern derby warrior. Banged one in and celebrated like he'd *ended the feud* single-handedly.
Shushed their fans. Pointed at the badge. Instant folklore.

🟦 Reda Johnson

Didn't care for finesse. He *cared about winning*.
Tackled anything in red that moved.
Left his mark — literally — on three United players in one game.
The fans adored him. So did the physios.

⚡ Jermaine Johnson

Wild. Unpredictable. Absolutely terrifying to defenders.
Scored a belter, backflipped into the corner flag, and nearly knocked himself out celebrating.
Still worth it.

🟦 Marcus Tudgay

Ice-cold finisher. The man *loved* playing United.
Every time he scored, it looked effortless. Every time he celebrated, it looked **personal**.

These players gave us **more than goals**.
They gave us **stories**.
Moments we'll never forget.

And for every derby win, every shushed away end, every late tackle that set the crowd off like a firework…

We say thank you.

True blue heroes.

CHAPTER 58: "MIND THE GAP!" AND OTHER FAMOUS CHANTS THAT DROVE THEM MAD

If there's one thing Wednesdayites do better than most — it's **get inside the opposition's heads**.

We don't just sing.
We **taunt, mock, tease, and turn pain into poetry** — and nowhere is that sharper than in a Steel City derby.

Here are the chants that drove United fans **completely round the bend** — and had Wednesday fans singing them in the bath for weeks.

☐ "Mind the Gap!"

Classic.
Used whenever United had a wobble — especially glorious during our spells above them in the league.

> "Mind the gap, Sheffield United…"
> *"Mind the gap, I say!"*

One year, someone made t-shirts. Another year, a lad turned up with a cardboard train station sign and stood on the tram stop singing it to every Blade he saw.

They hated it. Which made us sing it louder.

☐ "4–0 On Your Special Day"

Boxing Day. 1979. Never forgotten.
This chant reappears *every derby week* like clockwork.

> "Four–nil on your special day…"
> "You got battered by the Owls!"

Short. Sharp. Cuts deep.

There's even been a remix version with sleigh bells.

▫ "We Saw You Cry on Calendar News"

A direct hit.
Chanted after their cup exit in 2003 when their manager gave a teary-eyed interview on local TV.

We sang it so long, he actually banned interviews for a month.

▫ "You Fill Up My Senses – Like a Pound Shop Ronaldo"

OK, that one might've been aimed at a specific United player who tried five stepovers and fell over.
We rewrote the entire song. It went viral. Got banned. Made us love it even more.

▫ "You're Just a Pub Team in Rotherham"

Brutal geography joke. Especially popular when they flirted with relegation and got outnumbered by away fans in their own ground.

▫ "You're Red, You're Rubbish, You Haven't Had a Bath"

Old-school. Makes no sense. Still works. Got sung during a monsoon game. One Blade actually shouted, "I shower daily!" as a response. 3–1 to us that day. Spirit broken.

Because when you support Wednesday, chants aren't just noise.

They're **weapons**.
And we wield them with **gleeful pride**.

CHAPTER 59: THE ONE WHERE THEY THOUGHT THEY HAD US

There's no greater joy than seeing a Blade celebrate **too early**.

Because in derby history, some of our finest moments haven't come from dominating start to finish — they've come from those *late twists*, the *last laughs*, the *"I told you we'd do it"* moments.

Let's relive a few of the best times they thought they'd won... and we made them regret ever showing up.

☐ 1992 – The Comeback at the Lane

They were 1–0 up. Singing like they'd just won the FA Cup. We looked flat. The crowd, restless. Then — out of nowhere — John Sheridan picked up the ball, threaded a pass through red shirts like a needle through cloth, and BANG — equaliser.

Crowd erupted. Then, five minutes later — we won a corner. Waddle swung it in. Mayhem. It bounced off two defenders, one keeper, and finally over the line.

2–1 Wednesday.
Full-time whistle.
Their fans already halfway out of the ground.

One of ours held up a sign that read:

> "Told You We'd Nick It."

☐ 2009 – They Took the Lead. We Took the Points.

United scored early. Big celebrations. Big arms. Big chants.

Didn't last.

Tudgay equalised just before half-time. The Lane went quiet.

Then came the winner. A long ball. Flick-on. Smash.
We celebrated like we'd been holding our breath for *decades*.

Outside, their fans couldn't look us in the eye. One even said, *"You lot live for this, don't you?"*

He was right.

2012 – The "It's Never Over" Game

They were 2–0 up with 15 minutes left. Already singing "Easy! Easy!"

Big mistake.

We pulled one back through a scrappy rebound.
Then another — direct from a corner.
Stoppage time: they panicked, cleared it into Row Z.

But the damage was done.
2–2.
Their smugness wiped out.
We danced like we'd won the league.

In this rivalry, **momentum is everything** — and we *own* the comeback narrative.

We don't just beat them.
We **ruin** their afternoons.
And we do it **right at the end**.

Because they might start loud…
But Wednesday **always finishes louder**.

CHAPTER 60: IT'S MORE THAN FOOTBALL – WHY THE DERBY REALLY MATTERS

If you're not from Sheffield, you might not get it.

You might think this is just a game — a match on a fixture list. But if you're born in the Steel City, you know the truth:

This rivalry **is the city**.

From the minute you start school, it begins:

- **Blue or red?**
- **Hirst or Deane?**
- **Hillsborough or the Lane?**

Friendships are tested. Family WhatsApp groups go silent on matchweek.
You know where everyone stands — and you never *really* forgive them for choosing the other side.

The derby splits the city in half.
Pubs become battlegrounds. Workplaces tense up. Grandads stop talking to grandsons (temporarily).

But underneath the chaos, the chants, the constant need to remind them of 1979…

There's **respect**.

Because it means something. It means *everything*.
It's pride. It's identity. It's one side of the city telling the other:

> "We're here. We're louder. We matter more."

And when Wednesday win — whether it's a scrappy 1–0 or a beautiful 4–0 — it feels like the entire week glows brighter.

The bin men nod at you. The tram feels smoother. Your tea tastes better.

And if we lose?

We dust off the scarves, reload the songs, and remember every past derby where **they thought they had us... and we rose again**.

Because in this rivalry, there's only one thing more important than football:

Being Wednesday.

And in Sheffield — **that still means something.**

Always will.

PAGE 1: FAN VOICES – FROM HILLSBOROUGH TO THE WORLD

"My dad said: supporting Wednesday is like marriage — you don't walk away just because it gets hard. You stay, and sometimes that's the only thing that matters."
—*Joe, Crookes*

"I live in Australia now, but I still wake up at 2am to watch games. My neighbours think I'm mad. I am. I'm Wednesday. The badge doesn't come off with distance."
—*Rachel, Sydney*

"When I lost my job, I didn't tell anyone for weeks. Still went to every match. Still sang. Wednesday gave me purpose when I had none. The chant was the therapy I didn't know I needed."
—*Dean, Wadsley Bridge*

"My son was born on a matchday. I missed the game. Still sang 'Hi Ho Silver Lining' in the delivery room. My wife rolled her eyes. The midwife joined in."
—*Kev, Rotherham*

"It's not just 90 minutes. It's who I am. My grandad wore this scarf. My lad wears it now. Some people inherit wealth. I inherited blue and white."
—*Mo, Firth Park*

"I met my best mate in the away end at Blackpool. We bonded over dodgy chips and a last-minute equaliser. That was 15 years ago. Still mates. Still Owls."
—*Andy, Stocksbridge*

"My first tattoo was the Wednesday crest. My second was the date of my first win at Hillsborough. My third was a tactical error after 8 pints and a win at Barnsley. All worth

it."
—*Jess, Nether Edge*

"My mum doesn't like football. But she knits me a new blue-and-white scarf every time we make the playoffs. She's got more belief than the bookies."
—*Sam, Hillsborough*

PAGE 2: A WEDNESDAY BUCKET LIST

- Sit on the Kop and sing 'We Are Wednesday' until your voice breaks
- See us score in the first minute (or the 97th)
- Get rained on, frozen, and sunburnt — all in the same game
- Hear 30,000 people erupt in unison
- Win away at the Lane (and let the whole street know)
- Meet your hero in the car park and forget how to speak
- Watch a comeback that gives you goosebumps
- Buy a dodgy scarf from a man with no stall licence
- Lose your voice in the second half and still chant louder
- Share a Bovril with a stranger and call them family
- Hear a new chant start in Row Z and go viral by Row A
- Ride the tram with three generations of Wednesday fans in the same carriage
- Lose a bet, wear a mascot outfit, and still out-sing the other lot
- Watch a screamer fly in from 40 yards and say, "I knew he had it in him."
- Go pitchside for one game and feel like you've stepped into a dream
- Sit next to someone who's been coming since the 50s and realise you're part of something eternal

PAGE 3: LETTER TO MY YOUNGER WEDNESDAY SELF

Dear little Owl,

You're going to fall in love with a club that will break your heart and remake it stronger every season.

It'll teach you about loyalty when the league table says run. It'll show you what pride means when we lose on a Tuesday night in front of 6,000 and you still turn up Saturday.

You'll have your heroes. Waddle, Hirst, Windass, whoever your generation brings. One will make you cry. Another will make you believe again. Some will frustrate you so much you'll write angry letters you never send.

You'll swear we're cursed. Then you'll celebrate like a lunatic when we score a scrappy winner against a team in the bottom three. You'll hug strangers. You'll spill Bovril. You'll sing yourself hoarse.

You'll learn that football isn't always fair, and Wednesday definitely isn't always easy. But it's **ours**. It's muddy boots and cold seats and memories that outlive the players who made them.

And one day, you'll pass that scarf to someone younger. Maybe your kid. Maybe your mate's. Maybe just a stranger who needs it.

And when they ask why this club matters, you'll smile and say, **"Because it gave me everything I didn't know I needed."**

So keep believing, kid.

We are Wednesday. And that means something.

Forever.

PAGE 4: THE HILLSBOROUGH SOUNDTRACK – MUSIC THAT MADE US

A Wednesday matchday sounds like no other. It's more than chants and cheers — it's a living playlist that plays in every fan's head, every coach ride, every pub before kickoff.

Here's the **unofficial Hillsborough playlist** — each track tied to a memory, a moment, a match:

- **"Hi Ho Silver Lining" – Jeff Beck**
  The anthem. The warm-up, the winner, the war cry. You hear the opening riff and know you're home.
- **"Blue Moon" – The Marcels**
  The echo on a cold night match. That bit of class and melancholy in equal measure.
- **"Parklife" – Blur**
  Matchday chaos in a Britpop shell. Sung by everyone under 50 with a pint in hand.
- **"Don't Look Back in Anger" – Oasis**
  The long trip home after a heartbreaker. No lyrics hit like "So I start a revolution from my bed…"
- **"Great Escape Theme" – Elmer Bernstein**
  Played more times than we'd like to admit. But when it hits on the last day of the season, it becomes an anthem of survival.
- **"Three Lions" – Baddiel & Skinner**
  Hope. Disappointment. Repeat. Just like us. But we sing it anyway.
- **"We Are the Champions" – Queen**
  Usually sung ironically. Occasionally sung full voice, tears included.
- **"We Will Rock You" – Queen**
  The stomp. The clap. The pre-kickoff warning.
- **"Roll With It" – Oasis**

Because that's exactly what we do. Always have. Always will.

PAGE 5: MATCHDAY MEMES & WEDNESDAY BANTER

We may not always top the table, but we **own the banter league**. From group chats to fanzines to the back of toilet doors at S6, Wednesday humour is part coping mechanism, part cult classic.

Here's a selection from the meme-fuelled minds of Owl fandom:

☐ HEADLINE:
"Local Man Predicts 3–0 Win, Sees 0–5 Loss Instead, Still Says 'I Had a Feeling'."

☐ Photo Caption:
"This team's given me trust issues."

☐ Fan Tweet:
"Supporting Wednesday is like being in a long-distance relationship with someone who only texts when they lose."

☐ Fan Sign at Hillsborough:
"Don't worry lads. We'll get them in the playoffs. Probably."

☐ Matchday Food Review:
"Pie was cold. Chips were limp. Still better than the first half."

☐ Crowd Chant:
"We've had more managers than wins this year!"

☐ Post-loss excuse generator:
- Ref was blind
- Pitch was too dry
- Jupiter's in retrograde
- We're building for the future
- The WiFi in the dugout went down

☐ Announcer mix-up:

"Today's referee... hated by both teams equally."

Because we don't just suffer with style.

We **laugh through the losses**, roast our own players, and turn pain into punchlines faster than you can say "back pass."

That's Wednesday wit.
And nobody does it better.

PAGE 6: WHY WE STILL BELIEVE

We still believe — not because it's easy.
But because it's **ours**.

We believe when the score's 3–0 down.
When the league's upside down.
When the ref's had a howler and our striker couldn't hit a barn door with a beach ball.

We believe in last-minute goals and last-ditch tackles.
In youth team dreamers and 34-year-old loanees from Accrington.
In turning up, showing up, and standing up — no matter what the table says.

Because belief isn't about logic.
It's about **loyalty**.

It's about singing louder in defeat than in victory.
About hugging a stranger after a 1–1 draw that somehow meant everything.
About walking up Leppings Lane soaked through, freezing — and still smiling.

It's in the songs.
It's in the scarves.
It's in the blood.

This club isn't perfect.
But it's **ours**.

And that's why — through chaos, through comebacks, through Cup exits and crazy Tuesdays in March — we keep believing.

Because once you're Wednesday...

You're Wednesday forever.

MARTYN LEARY

Printed in Dunstable, United Kingdom